MW01265153

A Wretch Like Me

John Tunnell

Contents

1 WHERE DO I BEGIN?

As far as my family history goes I am not 100% positive about all the details. I will just tell you the parts I know. There are probably a lot of holes, but welcome to my life. I am not going to waste anyone's time, especially mine, grueling over non-important details. So, if something is a little off, I'm sorry. It isn't intentional. I'm not that smart.

So, it is my understanding that Mary, Queen of Scots is somewhere in my ancestry. Not really that important, but kind of interesting. Some great grandfather of mine during the civil war days invested some money in the railroad at the right time. He made some crazy amount of money like $800,000,000. I honestly don't know if that is in today's money or in real money back then. Either way, I mean, Wow! That's a lot of money. So, rumor has it that NOBODY in my family worked from then until my grandfather.

My grandfather was a foreign ambassador. He has been all over the world, he speaks at least 7 languages fluently, he is very decorated, and very intelligent. He divorced my grandmother when my mom was 14 years old right after her little sister was born. It is pretty sad really. It kind of made a mess of everyone. Who knows, maybe we were all a mess anyway.

When my mother was growing up she never lived in the same country for more than two years. She is also very intelligent. She speaks at least 5 languages fluently. She knows something about everything. I have to interject here and say that my mother is the most selfless person that I know. She truly has a good heart. I respect her more than anyone I have ever met in my life.

During the late 60's and early 70's she got involved with the hippie movement. At some point she met my father and she dropped out of college. They decided to backpack across Europe and Asia. I was conceived in India on their journey through the wilderness.

Apparently, she got pretty sick when I was in the womb and we both almost died. My parents got stuck in India for considerably longer than they wanted. My grandfather had to pull some strings just to get them out. So off we went to America. I was born at home in the woods in Seattle, Washington on April 5th, 1973 at 2:17 AM. My father had given himself and my mother hippie names. He was Sky Sheppard Surefoot. I think he had a bunch of other names in there too, but I don't know all of those. My mom became Dolphin Sheppard Surefoot. And I was born Sun Elk Sheppard Surefoot. His real name is Steve. My mother's real name is Pam.

Around that time my father was trying to dodge the draft so we kept moving around. My parents hitchhiked all over the place. I honestly don't know all the places we went. I do know that we had residence in Washington, Oregon, California, Hawaii, then back to Washington. Then my younger brother River Wisdom Sheppard Surefoot was born.

We moved around some more. My parents did a lot of drugs. We lived on a bunch of hippie communes. My father's mother committed suicide at some point. He got a little bit of insurance money ($10k) and wouldn't spend any of it on us kids. Instead he had found a pseudo-guru named Ocean who had a harem, claimed to be a God, beat his women, and did a lot of drugs. They both squandered the money. There was a lot of free love and a lot of acid. At some point Sky became violent.

Somewhere in the middle of this my younger sister was born, Wonder Faye Sheppard Surefoot. The last thing I remember about my father was a fit of rage that he had where he started throwing my blocks around and swinging a broom. I think he hit my mother. It is actually the only memory I have of my father. I told my mom about it a few years ago and she told me that that was the last time we ever saw Sky. I was about three years old. I never held it against him. I was never one of those kids that were mad at their dad for abandoning them. I never let it bother me. I was taken care of, and I figured that he had made some mistakes that could have happened to anyone...maybe even me one day. Who knows?

We went to visit my grandmother in Virginia and never came back. We just left everything and because of this we don't have any baby pictures or childhood memories. Once again, I never really gave it a second thought. I think we stayed with my grandmother for a little while. We must have had a falling out or maybe my mom just had gypsy feet from her upbringing. We moved to some hippie commune in Tennessee and then we moved to another one in Kentucky and then we moved to another one in Florida. At some point in all that I remember smoking weed. There was lots of weed everywhere. Stoners always feel like they are somehow being cool to get animals and kids high so it probably happened more than I can even remember.

left to right: John, John's Mom, River, Ann

My mother finally got burned out on the hippie lifestyle and moved in with my grandmother and aunt who were now living in Florida. In her defence, I really think that she embraced the free lifestyle, the healthy food, and the love and peace part of the hippie movement far more than the drugs. Once again, I could be wrong, but that was always the impression I got. So, we went to live with "normal" people for the first time in my life. That was a real adjustment for me. I was used to absolutely no rules at all and all of the sudden I was caught up in a completely uptight environment. I remember getting in trouble for peeing on the floor all the time! What can I say? I was a baby still, kind of.

My grandfather paid for us to get a condo in West Palm Beach, Florida. It was a 2-bedroom quadplex for my single mother and her three kids. The oldest of which was me and at the time. I had just turned five. I started kindergarten at a Catholic school six months late. It was no big deal because my mom had spent a lot of time with me already so I could already read and was way ahead of the game. The teacher used to leave and have me read stories to the other kids. At this point I had never had a haircut, so my hair was down to my waist. All the kids called me a girl and they made fun of my name a lot. I guess it bothered me enough that I got a little boy's haircut.

We went to day care for a year or so. I got picked on a lot because I was different. I don't know if money ran out or if I just volunteered for it, but pretty soon I was at home alone watching myself, and River, and Wonder. After another year or so it was decided that our lives would be easier if we had normal names. So we started being called John, Bill, and Ann.

In the second grade I moved to a different school. School was always really easy for me. I was the kid you hated in school. The one who never seemed to have to study, but always got straight A's. Yeah, that was me. I'm sorry about that. Even nerds have to have their achievements. River was decent in school, but not amazing. I don't know if he ever even cared.

Ann wasn't so good in school. She was held back in Kindergarten and then again in first grade. I think she was socially promoted after that. I could be wrong. If I would have known I was going to write a book 25 years later about the whole thing I might have paid more attention. I think my problem is that I am so completely self-absorbed that I don't pay much attention to all the details of others around me.

Anyway, Ann took the whole "not having a dad thing" worse than any of us. We were pretty mean to her when we were growing up. We always wanted to do boy things and we didn't want to be playing with Barbie dolls and stuff like that. We wanted G.I. Joe and Star Wars action figures. We wanted to make bike ramps and tree forts and play in dumpsters. We wanted to run and play until we hurt ourselves or we absolutely had to go home. As a result I am sorry to say that we were very mean to our little sister. I think it did permanent damage to her, and I am sorry for that.

Right before I started the fourth grade my mom started working as a secretary for this guy who was about to be a priest in the Catholic Church. He came over to our house a few times and the next thing you know I was in public school. I had been wearing a uniform to school for the last three and a half years and we just wore hand-me-downs to play in. I didn't know the first thing about dressing myself. I didn't understand social interaction with "normal" people. And by normal I mean cruel, heartless people. I was the biggest nerd in the world in the fourth grade. I was the nerd that even the nerds made fun of. Everyone else knew it and most importantly... I knew it. My self-esteem was shattered.

I got picked on every day. I didn't want to fight. I just wanted to go home and play outside. So this guy my mom was seeing had also been a marine for a lot of years. His dad had retired from the Army. They had been all over the world as well. He was a know-it-all. He was a bully. He was a hypocrite. He told me I had to defend myself. He told me to beat the bullies bloody. He told me to leave marks and do it in public where everyone can see. He told me to never stop hurting them until I was dragged off, and even then to keep trying to fight. He told me to fight dirty and mean. He told me that if I didn't fight back then I could expect a fight from him when I got home. He scared me, so I fought and I fought and I fought until the bullies stopped bothering me. In fact, I got in a lot of trouble and I think a lot of the kids thought I was crazy.

After 6 weeks in public school in Florida we all moved to Lake Charles, Louisiana. Chris married my mother at the Justice of the Peace. Me and River and Ann were there. We moved into a tiny two-bedroom apartment. Chris worked as a manager at Wendy's making something close to nothing. There were chemical plants nearby. They had sirens that would go off when there were too many hazardous materials in the air. Once again I got picked on a lot, so I got in a lot of fights. I got in a lot of trouble. Life was not good for me at all.

We lived in Lake Charles for a few months and then we moved to Georgia. This was now the third state that I had residence in and the fourth school I had gone to in one year. We moved to some white trash apartment complex. I got in fights all the time. Chris became more and more intolerable to me. From the time I was very young Everyone told me that I was the man of the house. I was told that I had to keep it together for everyone, so, I did... as well as I could, being a kid and all.

Chris drove me insane! He was uptight all the time. He was a neat freak. I have no problem keeping things clean, but I couldn't care less if I can bounce a quarter off of my bed when I make it or if my underwear is folded into perfect six-inch squares. He was strict about the stupidest things. He came in and immediately wanted us to call him Daddy. I was like "Who are you again? Oh yeah, the guy who is married to my mom now. I'm not impressed. I'm the man here, not you."

There were problems right away with Chris. So, to prove that he could be a good dad he adopted us. We had already been going by normal names for a while. But now because our names were going to change we could change them to anything we wanted. So in the fourth grade I was adopted and my name was legally changed. Of course, I wasn't too creative. I just stuck with the name I was already being called. The last name was a given, Tunnell. We got to choose our middle names. River chose Francis after St. Francis of Assisi because St. Francis liked animals and so did River. So he became William Francis Tunnell. Ann took my mother's middle name as her own, so she became Ann Mary Tunnell. I, on the other hand am an idiot! I had a monkey doll named Joe so I said just name me John Joe. They insisted on lengthening it so I am now John Joseph Tunnell.

Chris had a lot of what I considered to be stupid hobbies. He lifted weights. He knew everything about every battle and war throughout history. He knew karate. He read a lot! He was a pseudo-intellectual. He loved old black and white movies. He knew lots of details about the Catholic religion, since he had almost been ordained as a priest (until he met my mother). The worst hobby was that he played with these tiny little army men. They were each less than an inch tall. He would take pieces of plywood and put fake grass on them. Then he would make lakes and hills and battlefields with trees and brush and cannons, horses, and the like. All that by itself is cool, I guess. But we lived in a two-bedroom apartment and I was 9 years old, River was 7, and Ann was 6 and we all stayed at home by ourselves after school until they got home from work. It was pretty hard to avoid these huge pieces of plywood in the living room with tiny delicate men balanced all over them.

We messed those things up more than once and we had hell to pay every time. The really cool thing was that I still got to be the man of the house when it came to responsibility, just not when it came to authority. So, it didn't matter who did what while my parents were at work, I got the blame for it because I was the man. I was the one in charge. I remember one time in particular when Ann hadn't cleaned her room and I didn't make her. I went out to ride my bike. When I came home Chris grabbed me by my throat and lifted me up and threw me against the wall. He said "Why isn't your sister's room clean?" The whole time I was just thinking, "Who cares? It is going to be dirty again. Just lighten up a little. Is it really worth all this?" Stuff like that happened all the time.

So in the fifth grade we moved to Powder Springs, Georgia. We actually lived in a house for the first time in our life. It had a neighborhood and everything. Chris wanted to impress everyone. He re-enlisted in the Marine Corps. He got a bunch of credit cards and maxed them all out. We got all new furniture, new bedding, a new car, video games, stereos, TV's, all kinds of stuff. It was nice for a little while. I had a nice bike. That Christmas was probably the best in my life. We got so much stuff it was ridiculous!

The school I went to had bullies in it as usual, but I just went for the biggest one in the school. I beat him in front of everyone. I went ballistic. I beat him from one end of the hall to the other. I got him down on the ground and was just punching him over and over and over. I got dragged off by some of the guy teachers at the school. I got a few kicks in as they took me off of him. No one there ever messed with me again. I really didn't like fighting, but I had gotten pretty good at it. I realized that most of fighting was in the talking before the actual fight, not in the actual throwing of punches. The real goal was to intimidate the other person and make them feel inadequate. This way they would either back down, which means you win or they wouldn't fight as well because they were intimidated so you would probably win. Even if you lose everyone still respects you for not giving up. After you beat someone up they usually respect you and want to be your friend and so does everyone else. It is stupid, but true.

This has nothing to do with the story, but it is funny. One day I was at the bus stop by myself. There was some construction going on in the neighborhood. I saw a piece of lumber and a rock. I looked at the curb and thought, "Hmm, I could make a cool catapult." So I put a 1x4 on the curb. I put the rock on the bottom end of the board and I stomped on the other end of the board. Well, it didn't really work like I planned. The rock flew straight up and smacked me in the mouth. It chipped a piece off of one of my front teeth. I was so embarrassed I just spit it out and never told anyone about it until I was well into my twenties. Ok, back to the story.

Pretty soon Chris had a dream of owning a mobile home. We bought some land way out in the middle of nowhere. We paid way too much money to dig a well several hundred feet deep that never struck water. He dumped all kinds of money into this trailer idea. It never happened. We moved to Marietta, Georgia. I had to deal with bullies again. Nothing new. We moved into another two-bedroom apartment. I think we actually stayed there for almost a full year, which in case you haven't figured it out by now was monumental for us. River and I experimented a little with smoking. Nothing big, but it set the stage for what was to come. I started getting interested in girls. No big shocker. I was hitting puberty.

So, then we moved into Chris's sister's rent house in Fayetteville, Georgia. My mom thought that maybe if Chris could have a baby of his own then he could understand what being a father was really like and maybe he would be nicer to us. My mom got pregnant with my little brother Chris. He was born Feb. 8th, 1985. He was a lot of fun. I learned a lot about babies and children because of him. So my mother quit her job and started babysitting kids out of our house. Lots of them! I helped, because it was a lot of work for her. That poor woman was worn out, but she never gave up. I have always respected her.

Fayetteville wasn't all that bad really. Not too many bullies or maybe I was just getting used to it. Either way I was happy. There were some woods behind our house with a creek. We built forts, dug holes, swung on vines, swam, jumped in piles of leaves, played war, built ramps for our bikes and did every dangerous thing we could think of. It was great! I kissed my first girl. Also great! We played a lot of neighborhood sports. Nothing on a team, but still lots of fun! I spent seventh grade and part of the eighth grade in that house. That was a really long time to be in one place.

Half way through the eighth grade we moved to Kennedale, Texas. By this time I was actually being seen as kind of cool, which was nice. Nobody really messed with me too much. I started playing the guitar, which I loved (and still do). I noticed that everyone there seemed to do drugs. We had a rent house in a decent neighborhood. Chris was now a Gunnery Sergeant in the Marine Corps. He still drove me insane, but every once in a while he would do something kind of nice and I would think "Well, maybe he isn't that bad."

When I was younger and Chris would do something mean I would tell my mother and she would go to him and yell at him for it. I remember at some point I told her something he had done and she stopped me. She said something along the lines of "John, at some point you have to grow up and be a man. At some point you have to learn to stand up for yourself. You can't always hide behind me. And if you keep fighting Chris then you are in for some hard years ahead of you." That was the best and the worst thing my mom ever did for me. It was the worst because I used it as an excuse to do whatever I wanted. It was the best because it made me a man inside. I finally got cut loose and had to stand up for myself. I couldn't cower under my mother's wing any more. It was sink or swim. The cord had been cut.

As I started getting older I started getting all the speeches about sex and drugs and drinking and all that. Chris would always brag about all the drugs he had done and all the bad things that he had done. He bragged about all the girls he had slept with. It always sounded cool to me. Then he would change his mood and say that things were different now and that if I ever did drugs my life would be over. I could never get a job because they do lie detector tests now. So I would throw my entire life away, he would disown me, and he would beat me up. I was scared. I mean, I didn't want to do drugs anyway or any of that other stuff so it wasn't a big deal, but I knew if I ever did that it would all be over!

Well, as fate would have it I started hanging out with all the "cool kids". I discovered heavy metal music. I loved it! I started growing my hair out. At first I just listened to the innocent stuff like Bon Jovi and Stryper, Europe, and Cinderella. But I quickly moved to Iron Maiden, Metallica, Megadeth, Slayer, etc. As a young man I believed what I was told and I believed anything these bands said in their music. It consumed me. I held out for a few months, but one day River and I went out to a field with some of our friends. They had stolen cigarettes from their parents and we smoked them. So, I started smoking. I didn't even really like it. I just did it to be like everyone else. Tobacco is STUPID!

My parents started to accuse me of doing drugs and drinking. I really wasn't. I tried to defend myself, but they didn't believe anything that I said. So, finally I thought as long as I was getting accused of this I might as well do it.

So, I started drinking. This wasn't a big jump for me because Chris would drink all the time and he would insist on us trying beer and wine. I always thought alcohol was nasty, but it was different when you were with friends your own age. New year's eve, 1986 I got drunk and ended up in the bathroom with all the stoners, who were all my friends. Someone pulled out a sack of weed and everyone started getting high. So did I.

The first time it didn't really do anything. The second time it didn't really do anything. The third time I fell in love! I got high everyday after that. It was all I lived for. I became trouble overnight. First of all I hated my step-dad. School wasn't the least bit challenging. And I figured that since I had already thrown my life away and now I could never get a job or have a real life that I might as well learn to live like a criminal and enjoy myself. I cast off all restraint. I tried anything and everything that came my way. I was afraid of nothing and no one. I became the bully. I became everything that I hated.

I was never home. I always made lame excuses as to where I was. We would say we were staying at our friend's house. He would say he was staying at another friend's house, and that guy would say that he was staying at our house. My parents were having marital problems and they were busy with themselves so they didn't do much to stop me. Plus River and I shared a room that was a converted garage and it had it's own door to the outside. We would just say we were going to sleep and then sneak out and stay out all night. When my parents would find out about something they would try to put me on restriction or take something away. I couldn't have cared less. I had already given up on there being any hope of me being anything more than a drug addict. I figured I would die young, but I would have fun until then. I thought that when I died I would either cease to exist or be reincarnated as something. I couldn't control it so why bother even trying?

Somewhere in the middle of all this I died inside. I had been a straight A student my whole life. I had always been smart and good, but all that was gone now. This began the quick decent for me. River fell too, but not as hard as I did. I think he was just following his big brother and having a little fun. I actually **believed** what I said, which is what made me dangerous.

2   A WRETCH LIKE ME

I started to get in a lot of trouble in school. At first it was just detention. No big deal. I always had a great excuse as to why it was somebody else's fault than mine. My parents bought most of my lies. I would get in trouble, but they weren't home very much so it didn't really matter. Because I was only 14 years old money was hard to come by. It wasn't like I could get a job, but I needed money for drugs. I couldn't really ask my parents, so I discovered the fine art of stealing. I got good at it. I could pick pocket. I would steal stuff out of cars. I would break into houses and steal stuff. I would shoplift. I would steal anything that I could. It became a full time job for me.

There was this football player in my art class that showed me how to huff rubber cement. So, I spent some time trying cheap highs like that. I huffed glue, liquid paper, Freon, paint, gas, and anything else I thought would get me high. Huffing stuff like that left you with a big fat headache though, so I lost interest quickly.

There was this church girl in my art class who started rebelling against her parents. We met at some parties. She turned out to be a freak! I lost my virginity to her when I was 14 years old. So, I got that out of the way. We went out for a while. It wasn't good. After that I pretty much had sex with any girl that would let me. I didn't really have a girlfriend, just a bunch of intoxicated stoner sex. Nobody really cared about each other and it always ended badly. No big surprise.

As time went on school became less and less interesting for me, so I tried to make it more fun. I would wake up and get ready for school. At the bus stop I would get high. I would try to get out of classes so I could go get high. At lunch I would sneak off campus and go get high. In the afternoon I would be pretty baked so I would usually sleep in my afternoon classes. As soon as school got out I would go get high. And then for the rest of the day I would do everything in my power to go get high. It was ridiculous.

I was in trouble every day at school. They would ask me if I wanted swats or On Campus Suspension (OCS). For a few months I would take the swats everyday. It was over right away and I was tough, but after a while it started to hurt. I never got a chance to heal from the last swats I got and the coach that gave them to me started to hit me harder every time. Eventually, I chose OCS. I got 3 days. They sent a letter to my parents in the mail and my parents had to sign it and I could return it to the school. I intercepted the letter, stuffed it down my pants, forged their signatures, and brought it back to school. My parents never knew. I got out of OCS and got in a fight the same day. I don't even remember what it was about. So I got 5 more days in OCS. I got out and then got caught smoking on campus the same day. And so it went every day until they gave me OCS for the rest of the year!

I had forged signatures on all the letters so my unsuspecting parents didn't know anything. I did all my schoolwork for the rest of the year in just a few weeks. School was easy for me. Then I became bored at a whole new level. I thought, "What else are you going to do to me? I already have straight A's for the rest of the year. I already have OCS for the rest of the year. You can't hold me back and if you suspend me then I can just stay home, which isn't that bad. I'll just pretend to go to school and then come back home. You don't scare me." So, I just did as I pleased. I was out of control. We weren't allowed to talk or sleep or draw or move around. I didn't have any work to do, so I talked and drew pictures of Iron Maiden's mascot Eddie and slept every time my teacher wasn't looking. I was finally deemed a threat to regular OCS students, so they gave me my own room. Yes, I had an entire room dedicated to me. It was some kind of storage room before, but now it was my own private playground.

It was some kind of mess when I got through with it. I took all the desks and built a maze to the back of the room. I stacked them on top of each other almost to the ceiling. It took almost a full minute to get back to where I was. It was like having a cowbell on the teacher. They had given up on me anyway so they didn't really care. There was some Crisco oil in the room for some reason. I greased the entire chalkboard and, of course, ruined it. I carved all kinds of band names into the chalkboard like Ozzy, Metallica, Iron Maiden, and so on. It was covered. I had taken several of the chairs and turned them into a bed. Most of the time I would go get high and then go sleep on my "bed". I knew when my teacher was going to come and check on me so I would wake up and pretend to be doing something important when she showed up. I got to go to the bathroom a few times a day. I got to eat in the cafeteria, but I had to be by myself. Then she would tell me when it was time to go home.

After I learned her routine I would just leave campus and come back when she would check in on me. River was in the 7th grade at this point and he got OCS. They made the junior high kids come to the high school for OCS. Another friend of mine named Bruce was in OCS at the same time. I snuck out of my room and down to the regular OCS room one day. My teacher wasn't there. I did some stupid stuff like disconnect the PA speaker in their room and trip a breaker. I had locked the door in case she got there. Well, she got there. I hid in the closet for an hour until she went to the closet to get something. She jumped about two feet in the air when she saw me in there! Poor woman. I almost gave her a heart attack. It was so funny that I almost didn't care what my punishment was.

She made me stay in the main OCS room that day to keep an eye on me. Well, to pass the time we started passing notes. One of us would get up and pretend to sharpen our pencil and then drop a note on the other one's desk. This went on for a while. The note got really graphic. The note also made fun of the teacher. Bruce dropped it on my desk. I opened it up and started laughing out loud. The teacher had not been paying much attention, but she knew something wasn't right so she sent me out in the hall. I stuffed the note down my pants to hide it. She came out after a few minutes and said we had been passing drugs in class and for me to hand them over. I laughed at her, but I wouldn't tell her about the note. So, then I had to go to the office and explain myself to the principal. I told him that I didn't know what she was talking about. He insisted that everyone knew I did drugs and just to hand them over.

This went on all day. Finally, they called the police. We went through the whole thing again and I wouldn't break. So, they had to let me go. I thought it was so funny that the entire thing was just about a dumb note. If they had known what a big deal they had made out of it they would probably have felt pretty stupid. I didn't have anything better to do anyway, so it was almost fun for me. They couldn't have done anything anyway, even if they had found the note and nobody is going to stick their hand down some 14-year-old boy's pants unless they want to spend some time in jail. By this time in my life it was safe to say that I hated all authority and wasn't going to be told what to do by anyone.

Bruce and this other friend of ours, Jason, used to hang out all the time. Jason's dad cooked meth. Jason stole a lot of it from his dad who apparently didn't know the difference. It was worth about $5,000 roughly. I never saw the whole thing, but we always had lots of meth. We sold it and supported our habit. I gave some of it away to girls I wanted to have sex with. And we did most of it ourselves. I stayed up for weeks at a time. I didn't sleep or eat hardly at all. I would pretend to go to sleep, but since I couldn't sleep I would clean my room in the dark. I chewed the inside of my cheeks and lips up. Meth is nasty. For those of you who have never done it, don't! It tastes horrible! It is nasty in your nose or your mouth or however you ingest it. You can taste it the entire time you are tweaking. Coming down is painful all the way around. Plus it is very addictive.

Bruce, Jason, River, and I would go out all night, every night. We would steal whatever we could find, get as high as possible, and cause whatever problems we could. When we would get bored or tired we would break into an empty house and mess it up pretty bad. We would crank the heat up all the way. We would clog the toilets. We would start fires. We would vandalize. We were mean. Whoever fell asleep first in our group was in for it. We would light their shoes on fire, pour pancake syrup in their ears, put jalapeño juice on their lips, pour beer on them, throw things at them, stick hair in their nose, or any other mean thing we could think of.

All the people I hung out with were into heavy metal music. There was a lot of Satanism and cultish stuff going on in my circle of friends. I was curious, so I dabbled a little bit. I remember I had heard about this demon that you could pray to and he would give you whatever you wanted, but then he would take it back from you in pain. We were going around stealing stuff one night in Kennedale out of someone's garage. There were about 6 of us. We stole a scooter with a flat tire, a stereo, and some other stupid stuff. It was the middle of the night and we were on a main road, on foot, with all this stuff. It looked very suspicious. Plus, we had made a lot of noise and I'm pretty sure the homeowner's had called the police on us.

All of the sudden there was a cop car right behind us. We were still a few miles away from the Arlington/ Kennedale border. So, I prayed to this demon that we would get away from this cop, because I knew we were busted. We all started running. We stayed on the road instead of running off the beaten path and the cop was right behind us in his car the whole time. We ran for a long time. We finally got to Arlington and then we ran into a field full of cows. The cop never caught us! It didn't make any sense. There was no reason why he shouldn't have caught us. Either way, we were safe and I was happy until the next day when I got sick for no reason at all. I had a terrible stomach ache like never before. That demon took it back from me in pain.

There was another time that my family was going out of town to Washington State. I didn't know if I could go a whole week without getting high, but it looked like there was no way around going on this dreaded trip. So, once again I prayed to this demon that I wouldn't have to go. At the last minute, in the airport, my mom said if I could get a ride home then I wouldn't have to go. I called a friend and miraculously got a ride. I had a non-stop party for the whole week they were gone. I met some girl. We had a lot of sex. I was in drug heaven for a solid week. A week later my mom came home. I got some weird rash all over me and I had a super high fever. I was in my bed for exactly one week. It was miserable! These are just a few examples of satanic stuff I did. I did lots of stuff like that though.

I did a lot of destructive things as well. I burned down half of some house I broke into. River burned two different fields, someone's yard, and part of their house. If there was anything we were good at though it was running, oh yeah, and making up lies. We ran from the cops so many times I can't even count it any more. To be honest most of the stuff we messed up was totally random. It just happened to be there when we felt like destruction. One day we were walking to the movies. Jason saw a line of cars coming at us and he said you know if you wait until there is another huge line of cars and then throw a rock at the window of the first car they won't be able to stop in time and we can get away. So, without a thought I grabbed a rock and waited for the next string of cars. When they came, I threw the rock out into traffic. It smacked some guy's windshield really hard. CRACK! It was loud! We ran to the nearest street and turned every corner until we had lost them for sure. We kept walking towards the movies on the back roads. We were pulling signs up out of people's yards and throwing them everywhere. We were tearing off people's mailboxes and putting them down the road in someone else's yard. After a while we had to get back on the main road. I had completely forgotten about the rock. This car screeched to a halt right in front of us. I thought, "Do I know someone in a white car like that?" Then he jumped out and said "Freeze, get up against the wall."

I didn't know what was up, but I looked at River and Jason and turned around and ran. I didn't "freeze" for anyone! I assumed they would be right behind me. I ran fast and hard. When you run you can't really look back or else you will get caught so I just looked straight ahead and ran like there was no tomorrow. After a while it sounded quiet behind me, I ducked into a Taco Bueno, went right to the back in a corner that wasn't visible from the road, and hid until it was safe. River and Jason were nowhere to be found, but I figured they just ran a different way and I would meet up with them in a little while at the movies.

They never showed up, so finally I called my mom to give me a ride home. She asked why I had thrown a rock through some guy's windshield. I played dumb. Then I said, "How do they know it was us, anyway? He is just blaming us because we have long hair and heavy metal T-shirts on. How unfair!" Well, I thought it was a pretty weak excuse, but it worked. River and Jason had both been arrested. The car I hit was an off duty cop. What are the odds of that? But, we got away with it. Years later I casually mentioned the whole thing to my mother and she still believed that we hadn't done it. Poor Mom. I was such a liar.

We would also shoplift all the time, mostly tapes, magazines, and food. We were small time in the worst way. One day I was stealing "Diary of a Madman" from Ozzy from a K-mart. Some old lady saw me stealing and told the manager of the store. They got security and brought me to the front of the store. I had put the tape down my pants. They called the cops and the cops were on their way when I just wriggled out of their arms and ran out of the store. Some of the guys chased me for a little while, but you aren't going to catch a drug addict kid on speed that is basically running for his life. They had rules to follow and people to answer to. I, on the other hand, just had to get away. Needless to say, I got away again.

One night about twenty of us stoner metal heads were walking around in a back alley. Several trucks pulled up and started yelling stuff at us like they wanted to fight. Without hesitation every one of us pulled out our knives and started walking towards them. They were rich and had nice cars so they felt superior. We, on the other hand, were poor and mean and had nothing to lose. I thought "Well, I guess I'm going to have to kill someone tonight." Fortunately for everyone we must have psyched them out pretty bad with our absence of fear so they yelled some rude things and then drove off. I was pretty relieved. I didn't want to have to kill anyone, but the sad thing is that I would have. You would think this would be a lowest point of my life experience where I would ask, "What have I become" and change for the better. Nope. It didn't affect me at all. I just kept on going like it was nothing.

Well, eventually my parents figured out that I was getting into a lot of trouble. So, they took away what they thought the root of the trouble was, my long hair. The root of my trouble was that I was bored and angry and I could never measure up to my step-father's ridiculous demands. Nothing I ever did was good enough for him. I got straight A's. I was smart. I was clean. I was responsible. I did everything I was told. But still, I was always just short of pleasing him. I was good, just not good enough. So, I gave up trying. I hated that man. When they cut my hair I walked out of the barbershop and saw my reflection in the mirror. I was so upset that I decided to leave and never come back. So, right at that very moment I turned and ran. I ran and ran and ran. My mom saw me and tried to catch me. She couldn't keep up. She yelled after me to come back, but I didn't. I ran through fields and woods. I didn't stop running for almost an hour.

I got my ear pierced, which Chris had forbidden me to do. I slept in some girl's closet that night right down the street from my house. I spent the next few days out in fields. I got pretty hungry. Being a runaway is not very glamorous! After four days I made up a list of things that I needed from home to survive: food, toothbrush, toilet paper, music, toothpaste, money, etc. I went up to the junior high during recess to give the list to River. The principal saw me and started chasing me. I have to give that guy credit he chased me for quite a while. I jumped over fences and ran through people's backyards. He stayed right behind me for a while too. Of course I got away. I hung out for the rest of the day out in some woods close to the school.

I waited for the buses to come and then ran up to give the list to River through the school bus window. Well, as I was doing that I heard my least favorite phrase, "Freeze! Police!" Of course "freeze" translated to "run" for me, so I started running. Then another cop car pulled in front of me. So I turned and started running another direction. Everywhere I turned there were cops. I wasn't going to let that stop me. I just kept running until one of them said, "Freeze, or I will shoot you!" Now I know as well as you that he probably wouldn't have actually shot me over being a runaway, but we were in Podunk Texas and this guy sounded serious so I stopped. That was the first time I got arrested. They got a statement from me that consisted of some ridiculous string of lies and inconsistencies.

My parents came and picked me up from the police station. They were quiet for most of the ride home. Then Chris said, "So, John, how long have you been doing drugs?" I of course denied doing any drugs and said I was just tired of him and I was mad because they had cut my hair. Which was partly true. The reason I didn't have any drugs on me when they arrested me was because I was out of drugs at the time. After all, I had been on the run for 4 days with no money. My parents thought that if they gave me a little more freedom I would be all right. Nope. It was way too late for that. They gave an inch. I took a mile.

One night my friend Bruce tried to kill himself. He drank a fifth of a gallon of Southern Comfort and took several grams of meth. He had tried to call me to see if I wanted to "go" with him. I'm so glad I didn't get that call. Bruce survived. I can't say for sure, but I might have actually done it too.

I had another friend named Danny who moved away. A few weeks later we got news that he had killed himself by drinking a bunch of anti-freeze. As you can imagine news like this became more and more frequent as time went on. How did I not get it? There are a few ways out of this lifestyle: you die, you go to jail, or you quit. If those were my options, I chose death.

Then the summer after 9th grade came. I was out of control. Chris did something to River and Ann one day when I was gone. My mom asked us if she should divorce Chris. We all told her yes. We all hated him. In my mind he was one of the main reasons why I had become such a mess in the first place. So, we moved out of the house into another two-bedroom apartment in Arlington. I was such a jerk I insisted on River and I sharing the master bedroom and I made my mom, Ann, and little Chris stay in the small bedroom. My mom got a job as a reservationist at American Airlines. So, my now single mom supported 4 kids by herself while making $7.50 an hour. Wow! That must have so difficult for her! The three old ones were hellions, and then she had an infant to take care of as well. I don't know how she did it.

She worked at night. Conveniently, so did I, well if you want to call it work? She woke up around 4 or 5 in the afternoon. I made sure to wake up a little before her so that it looked like I had been up all day. Then she went to work and I went out to steal and get high. One night these skaters wanted us to steal a quarter pipe skateboard ramp for them. They said they would give us $50 for it. So at three o' clock in the morning River, Russell, Dave, and I all walked across several highways to another neighborhood. We each grabbed a corner of this huge ramp. We walked it through the neighborhood, across a two-lane access road, across a five-lane highway, through a huge ditch, across another five-lane highway, across another two-lane access road, and into a hiding spot in some bushes. I would like to interject and say that you can make a lot more money being honest than you can stealing. When you figure all the planning, the risk, the time, and the low return on stealing the average thief makes way below minimum wage.

So, after my regular routine of causing trouble all night I would come in just before the sun came up and jump in bed and pretend to be asleep when my mom got home from work. One night I wasn't paying attention to the time and I was about to be late. I actually saw my mom driving down the highway towards the apartment. I ran, barely missed her, and climbed up the balcony while she was going up the stairs, jumped in bed fully clothed right before she opened my bedroom door to see me sleeping quietly just as I should have been. That was close! Welcome to my life, an inch away from disaster at any given moment.

Life became more and more boring for me, so I started seeking more and more thrills. We used to walk down to this bridge and jump off of it into the water below. That was fun! I did that as much as I could. One day I had a girl all the way naked down in the water with me when the cops came. We hid in a storm drain for a while, but they figured out we were down there. Her bathing suit had gone down stream somewhere and we couldn't find it. So I let her wear my shirt. It was white and we were both all wet. We had to have the cops drive us home with her wearing nothing but a white T-shirt. I was a real jerk.

I got pretty good at art and music. This music store had a "Create an Eddie" contest. Eddie is the mascot for Iron Maiden. I made two clay sculptures and painted them. I made "Can I Play With Madness" and "Piece Of Mind". I won the grand prize! River and I got front row tickets, back stage passes, all their albums, autographs, picks, drumsticks, and our pictures taken with the band. It was amazing! It was like a dream come true for me. They were my heroes. I was so high when I met them that I missed out on the whole experience.

At some point Ann figured out that River and I were doing drugs and lots of them. I really didn't think it was a big mystery, but I guess it shocked her. She told my mom and my mom threatened to call the cops on me if I ever got high again. It was right before school started and I thought long and hard about it for a few minutes. I knew that if I ran away again that I would become a dropout and that I would never go back to school. Well, I left anyway. I chose drugs over any real life. Why? Because when you are addicted to something you can't imagine living without it and you will pay any price for it and defend it at any price.

So, River and I ran away again. Several days went by. One night we slept under a bridge overpass until the ant bites were too much to take. Another night we slept behind a dumpster until early in the morning when the dump truck came to pick up the dumpster. We heard the loud beeping of the truck and the bright lights flashing in our faces. Startled, we jumped over the fence behind the dumpster. Another night we slept in some lawn furniture by a swimming pool in a nearby apartment complex. We slept on a few friends' floors, a few closets, some bathrooms. How uncomfortable! We ended up at some party and later that night we stayed at this guy Tony's house. His parents asked a lot of questions. We lied and just said we were staying the night. They didn't buy it. So then we said that our step-dad was beating us, which was kind of true. He was pretty rough. They said if he is so bad that we should tell the police. I didn't think that was a good idea at all. I HATED COPS! Plus, I was a runaway.

They assured us that they would be cool and just let us stay the night as long as we went home the next day. I told them that I would, which was a lie. We went back to Tony's room and a few minutes later a cop was knocking on his bedroom door. He listened to our bogus stories for a minute and then he handcuffed us, arrested us, and took us to jail. I was going to jump through Tony's window and try to run, but there was a huge tree and a bunch of bushes right in the way so I figured I would just hurt myself and they would still catch me. We stayed the night in jail. Then my mom came to get us. The cops handcuffed us again and put us in the back of the cop car. Normally they didn't do that to take you home? They just let your parents have you.

I started to think something was up. The cop started driving the wrong way home. I started kicking the back of the cop's seat and tried to get out. We pulled up at Millwood hospital, which I soon learned was a rehab. They started booking me. My eyes rolled back in my head. I started hissing and cussing and yelling obscenities at everyone. I fought all the way in. Through every door and every hall that led me there I kicked and fought. It was a little tough since I was greatly outnumbered and I was handcuffed. So they put me in a room and told me to take my shoes off. I told them I wanted to see a lawyer. They couldn't keep me here! I wanted out and I wasn't taking my shoes off or doing anything else they told me to do! They had better let me go.

All of the sudden six huge weightlifter guys came into my room and told me to take my shoes off. Used to bullies, I told them the same thing I told the other guys and the cops. A split second later they each grabbed one of my limbs. I grabbed the doorknob and fought them all off for several minutes. I put up a good fight. One guy grabbed one of my arms. Another guy grabbed the other one. A guy grabbed a leg. Another one grabbed my other leg. One sat on my back. And one sat on my head. I had three long earrings in at the time. While they strapped me down to the bed the guy sitting on my head ripped out all three of my earrings. There was blood all over my pillow. They finally finished strapping me down and left. I think they took my shoes off just to show me that they had won.

As soon as they left, I bit open one of my hand restraints, undid my other hand restraint, reached down and loosened my leg restraints, and slithered through the one holding my waist. I looked for a way out of the room. There wasn't one. So, I just beat on the door and told them that they couldn't keep me inside here or anywhere else for that matter. I was getting out, so they might as well cooperate! A few minutes later they opened the door with the same guys who proceeded to strap me to the bed again. Only this time they tied me in tight and used extra restraints. Once they left again I got out of the hand and feet restraints, but I just left the one around my waist and went to sleep. I was tired anyway.

I was strapped to that bed all night and all the next day. Finally a guy came in and said " John, how long have you been doing drugs?" I lifted up my head, turned to him, looked him in the eye, and said "I don't do drugs." Then I turned back over and went back to sleep. I didn't know who this was and I didn't care. I wouldn't be here long enough to get to know anyone here. They had no proof. I didn't have any drugs on me. I would be out in no time. So they left me there for the better part of that day.

Someone finally came in and asked if I was hungry. I told him I had to go to the bathroom so could I get untied now. He asked if I was done fighting. I thought for a minute about how bad I had to go and I agreed not to fight him. So they untied me. They gave me some food. Which was probably underwhelming food, but because I was so hungry it tasted great to me. So, after a while they let me take a shower, de-liced me, did a strip search, and let me out into the general population.

I just figured that this is what rehab was like. I was prepared for the worst. I thought River went through the same thing. Nope, I was wrong. River was hitting on girls, shooting pool, watching TV, playing foosball, and eating well. Not only that, but he had given them some sob story about how he had gotten sucked into the drug world and he wanted to get out. He was out of rehab in less than two days. I was in for seven weeks. At first I denied that I even did drugs at all. But everyone had already spilled the beans and I guess it was pretty obvious to everyone.

After it had been established that I did actually get high. Then they realized that I got high ALL the time! So, I stopped denying it and I just said, "Yeah, I get high and I'm not going to quit. I will get high until I die. I love it!"

Everything in rehab is therapy. You have school therapy, group therapy, family therapy, physical therapy, recreational therapy, food therapy, art therapy, one on one therapy, and so on. It wore me out. I just wanted to be left alone. The people in there were freaks! There was one guy who had been in hospitals for the better part of his life. He was addicted to **sugar**, of all things. He got hold of a huge bag of cookies one day and ate the whole thing. Then he started bouncing off the walls until they took him away. I think he was just lonely and starving for attention. What kind of parent can institutionalize their child for being addicted to sugar?

The girls were mostly there for depression, suicide attempts, and eating disorders. There were a lot of messed up people in there. They put me in this room with a huge, black, mentally challenged guy named Howard. Every time I walked into my room he was buck naked and masturbating in the middle of the room. It was so disturbing! That guy freaked me out!
In retrospect, I did learn a few important lessons in rehab though.

This one counselor said, "How do you quit doing drugs?" Someone said just stop doing them. He said, "How do you know when you have stopped doing something? How long do you have to go before you know that you have actually *quit* something? He said that you had to have an achievable goal or else how will you know when you have gotten there. He also said that you have to have something positive to be going towards so that you can go away from the drugs, or whatever your bad habits were." That actually made sense to me. There was a minute that I thought maybe one day I would grow up and help kids like this guy. Then I remembered that I was a loser, and I gave that up pretty quickly.

I met a girl in rehab named Michele. She told me just to tell the rehab what they wanted to hear and I would be out in no time. So, I learned how to tell the people what they wanted to hear. Not a great lesson, I admit, but it got me out of rehab pretty quickly. After a week of telling everyone how much I wanted to change my ways they were convinced and I went up to the next level in a different hall. This got me out of Howard's room. A week after that I was out of rehab all together. I thought, man that was quick. Later, I learned that my mom's insurance had run out and I had already racked up a $40,000 bill there so they released me because we were out of cash. It is amazing how quickly patients are "cured" once their insurance runs out.

Well, at the time I didn't know that. I was such a good liar that I convinced myself that I really wanted to quit drugs. Plus, I was seeing this girl, Michele, from rehab that wanted me to stay clean. As long as we stayed together, I stayed off drugs. Then she told me that she was pregnant and that she thought it was her ex-boyfriend's. I did the math and unless she was cheating on me it was mine. Well, she had been cheating on me. After that day I never saw her again.

"When an impure spirit comes out of a person, it goes through arid places seeking rest and does not find it. Then it says, 'I will return to the house I left.' When it arrives, it finds the house unoccupied, swept clean and put in order. Then it goes and takes with it seven other spirits more wicked than itself, and they go in and live there. And the final condition of that person is worse than the first."

- Matthew 12: 43-45

That old house was me. I went back to drugs that same day with a vengeance. I never looked back. My seven demons and I headed for destruction... full speed ahead!

3 THE ROAD TO HELL

One of the first things I did when I got of rehab was try to find Tony, the guy whose parents called the cops on me and got me put in rehab in the first place. We were driving close to his house and I said, "Let's go get Tony. I'm going to kill that guy." The person driving me said "Man, you are too late he's already dead! He was huffing Freon out of an air conditioner and he froze his lungs and died. They found him naked, blue, and dead in his room." His death should have hit home, but it didn't. I felt bad for saying I wanted to kill him, but not that bad. I didn't even give a second thought to quitting drugs or even to quitting Freon. I am so stupid!

I had spent the first 6 weeks of 10th grade in rehab, but while I was in rehab my mother moved so now I went to yet another new school, Martin High School. This school had lots of money. There were several thousand students there so I just blended in and did my thing. I don't even think I got in any fights. I could be wrong, it all blends after a while.

I fell in with some druggie friends and started getting high again. I had been clean for about 10 weeks. The first few times I got high I just got a headache, but then it kicked in and I fell in love again. I loved the escape of it. I loved the thrill of it. I loved the danger and the risk. I loved feeling different. I loved everything about being high. It was a slice of heaven to me that I never wanted to leave. I quickly moved up from the petty stuff I had been doing too much bigger doses and bigger deals.

6 weeks later we moved to a duplex in another part of Arlington and I went to yet another school. I met a guy who had a brother that was a big time dealer. He would get me lots of weed. I was going through several ounces a week, personally! For the first time in my life my grades actually started slipping. I had always been the guy that didn't have to study and still got straight A's. I had Biology right after lunch and I was always so incredibly high for that class that I just slept. I still managed to get a 69 for the 6 weeks, which was barely an F. I had actually gotten an F, and I didn't care one bit.

I was partying hard! I didn't care about anyone or anything. I would go across the street from Arlington High to get stoned or buy or sell drugs. It is amazing how much drug use goes on all around us everyday that we are oblivious to. A friend of mine had a brother that was in love with acid. I wanted to do acid really bad. He finally let me have some. The first time it didn't do anything.

I was talking about it to a friend of mine and someone overheard the conversation. They said two things that stuck out to me: 1) " Acid is dangerous! It is made with strychnine, which is rat poison. You take more than two hits and it could kill you." and 2) " I know a guy named John who got into acid. He overdosed and now he is a Christian. Now he preaches to people all the time. He is up in the northwest somewhere in the woods." I thought he was an idiot at the time, but for whatever reason what he had said stuck with me.

I didn't care. That would never happen to me. I would never be a Christian. I hated those people! What a bunch of hypocrites! Hiding behind their religion, afraid to do anything fun. I was going to do whatever in the world I felt like doing and nobody, and I mean nobody was going to stop me!

So, I got a hold of another hit of acid and I ate it. A bunch of us had gone out to the woods. There was a huge swing someone had put across this creek. One side was a lot higher than the other. We had just gotten high again and we were running through the woods when the acid hit me for the first time. This acid I had taken was called Dancing Test Tubes.

Acid is the most indescribable experience in the world. It is like trying to explain a dream to someone. Unless you were there it just doesn't make sense, and of course who can be there with you inside your head? You are the only one who sees what you see. It is as if all your senses just got cross-wired. You see the world like you have never seen it before. Everything is fluid. The walls breathe. The grass and the trees grow right in front of you. The floor crawls. Everything around you is alive and doing something different. You can't possibly take it all in! It is total sensory overload!

The first thing I noticed was that acid affected ALL your senses not just your sight. I had always heard that you saw weird things, like watching a movie or something. You stood on the outside and watched the show. That isn't true at all. You are sucked right in! You hear weird things that aren't there, things you can't even imagine... until you have done it. Of course you see things, lots of things. Your mind turns into a huge brainless stew of everything you can't even imagine. Your taste is different. Your smells are different and bizarre. Everything you feel is foreign. It is like being in another world! It is like leaving earth and never really coming back.

They say that you never come down off of acid, that you just get used to it... and I believe that. Every other drug goes through your bloodstream and eventually washes out through your kidneys. It might take 6 months, but eventually it is gone. Not so with hallucinogens. They go to your nervous system, to your brain, and to your spinal cord. They can do a spinal tap on you 50 years later and it will still be there. If you have ever done it you know what I am talking about. If not, just take my word for it.

The other thing you do is laugh for no reason at all ... for hours. Until your whole face just hurts from laughing, and then you laugh some more. I can't describe what I saw out in the woods that day. I know that I smoked a half-ounce of weed that day and at some point I realized I just can't get any higher, but I couldn't sleep because of the acid. I LOVED IT! Coming down was rough though! It feels like your whole body is sore and tense and in pain. Plus the real world starts kind of coming back, which is no fun at all! I was so paranoid when I went back home that night. I thought it was written all over me. I thought everyone knew what I had done. I had crossed a line for sure. The next day I realized that someone had stolen all my money and a huge sack of weed from me while I was tripping on acid. I was so mad!

I became one of the biggest drug pushers around. I wanted everyone to get high all the time. I shudder to think of how many people I actually convinced to do drugs. It is a big number. In just a few weeks I had gone from doing no drugs at all to doing everything I could get my hands on. I got my first job at Chuck E. Cheese Pizza, in Arlington. I cooked pizzas, washed dishes, dressed up as all the Chuck E. Cheese characters, and sold drugs. There was no time when I was awake that I wasn't high. Any drug that came along was fair game to me. I was afraid of nothing and no one.

I was taking enough meth to stay up for weeks at a time. I was smoking a half-ounce of weed a day (about $50 at the time). And I started taking acid every chance I got. I quickly moved up to taking 4 or 5 hits at a time, several times a week. I would have done it more, but I soon realized that if I did it too much it wouldn't have any effect since I had built up such a tolerance. So, I could only go 3 or 4 times a week. I had hook-ups with big time dealers and I quickly realized that I could support my habit easier if I sold drugs. I was already pushing them, so I might as well make some money at it. I made quite a bit of money, but I spent it all on drugs so all I really did was support my habit.

After a little while I got fired from Chuck E. Cheese's. They said I had stolen a hot dog for another employee. Everyone did that, though. I had sold meth to my manager and I think he told someone else. It was pretty obvious what was going on though. Every 30 minutes or so some long haired greasy looking guy would come up to my job and ask for me, we would go to the bathroom for a few minutes, and then he would leave. I always had lots of cash and I was only making $3.50 an hour. I was always willing to take the trash out back and I always came back looking slightly more baked then when I left a few minutes before. Anyway, I got fired. I didn't really care that much. It was just a cover anyway.

One day my mom came home early from work and I was at home tripping on acid. We talked for about an hour. I know I had to have said some pretty stupid things because I was lost in space at the time. My mom had done a lot of drugs earlier and I knew she knew what was up. I just figured she was being cool about the whole thing. She had caught me high and drunk too many times. Finally, she told me that if she saw me high one more time that she would call the police on me.

I know that she was under a lot of stress at the time. She was a single mom making almost nothing with 4 kids to support. Three of which had already been in rehab and were some of the biggest problem children in the area. And the other one, Chris, was still an infant. Looking back, I don't know how I could have been so cruel and selfish. Especially considering how wonderful of a mom she had always been to me. I'm sure what she had said was just an idle threat, but what she didn't know was that I had a quarter pound of weed and a sheet of acid in my guitar case. That was a lot of drugs. That was enough to get me in some serious trouble. I had heard the punishment (at the time) was one year in prison for each hit of acid you had on you AND if there was intent to sell, which there was, then it became manslaughter.

I didn't take any chances. That night I told my mother whatever in the world she wanted to hear, went to my room, packed my things, and snuck out of my window. I ran away again. This was the last time, though. I walked for miles and miles and miles. I was homeless for a little while. I took the drugs I had and turned them into money and then bought more drugs with it. Because I always had drugs, I miraculously always had a ride.

My friend Russell and I were going in halves for all the drug dealing. I was fifteen and he was seventeen. We had this dealer that we were buying our weed from. He would sell us a pound for about $800. We would divide it into 64 quarter ounce bags, make each bag just a little light, keep the extra for us and sell the quarters. We would make about $1600 off of a pound of weed. We would also sell acid, meth, cocaine, pills, and once again anything that we could get our hands on. It was good money for a homeless kid. Especially when you figure we were selling about a pound a week or more plus all the other stuff.

So, anyway this dealer we bought from always freaked me out. He had guns everywhere and was always on edge. He was really paranoid. There were always lots of people at his apartment and there were bricks of marijuana everywhere. One day we had run low so we were going up to his door to get another pound. We had a lot of cash on us and we were about ten feet away from his door when the door busted open and cops came out of his apartment struggling with him. They were handcuffing him right there in front of us. If we had come one minute earlier it would have been us going to jail too. We just turned around and kept walking and acted like we didn't know the guy. That was just one of about a hundred close calls that happened to me.

Another time we had almost run out of money and these two teenagers said they knew somebody that would buy everything we had. We agreed to meet them in the football field of this junior high school at midnight. Four big guys showed up. They threw us up against the bleachers and frisked us. I was thinking what in the world are you doing, are you guys cops? They pulled out guns and knives and threw us on the ground. They put a knife to my throat and a gun to my head and made me give them all my drugs and all my money. They did the same thing to Russell. The two guys that set the whole thing up started screaming like little girls and tried to run away. The big guys caught them and beat them up a little. They were crying and screaming for mercy. It was pathetic.

The only thing I could think was "Man this is no good. Now we won't have any drugs or any money! How are we going to make it?" I tried to hide some of it, but they found everything we had. Then they stood us up and got behind us. They threatened us a little and then told us to run as fast as we could. They said if we turned around they would shoot us. I really didn't believe them. The two cowards started running as soon as they let them go. Russell was right behind them. I didn't want to be the only one left behind so I ran too. I was so mad.

When dealers rob other dealers it isn't like we can go tell the cops or anything. "Uh, yes officer those goes stole my drugs and my drug money. Go get them for me." Fortunately Russell had a job and his last check came in right after that. It was enough to get us back on our feet again. I was thankful.

Shortly after that we moved in with this girl named Jane. She had a baby. At first we were just sleeping on the floor, but there wasn't much room in her apartment and pretty soon I was sharing the sofa bed with her. We started having sex shortly after we moved in. Once we had an actual place to sell drugs, our sales went through the roof. We had so many people coming through everyday we got evicted from 5 apartment complexes and a mobile home trailer park in less than 6 months. We were big time dealers. I got a job at a burger place, probably because Jane was working there.

I was pretty late for work one day and my manager showed up at our trailer. It was hot and we refused to turn on the air-conditioning so the front door was open. I was asleep in our room in the back. He walked right in and back to my room. Everyone else in the place was shooting up, except me. So there were needles all over the place. Every kind of drug paraphernalia was lying around that place. In my room alone there was a set of scales with a pound of weed just sitting out waiting to be quartered up. He woke me up and told me that he was also a narcotics officer. He said that because he had come in without a warrant that he couldn't pursue prosecuting me this time, but that I should watch my back. I did get fired, but I didn't go to jail.

We had lots of stolen stuff in our place because drug people quickly run out of money so they start bringing anything else they can get their hands on. We had a whole room dedicated to stolen stuff. We had radar detectors, TV's, VCR's, stereos, guitars, amps, electronics, and every other gadget that was out at the time. Someone had stolen a guitar from a blind guy and traded us for drugs. One day the captain of the Kennedale Police Department came and paid me a visit. He knew about the guitar and apparently he knew about everything else as well. He threatened to arrest me. I played dumb, so he legally couldn't do anything. He made sure I returned the guitar to the blind guy through someone else. So, I did.

A few weeks later we noticed that a police helicopter seemed to be circling right above our mobile home. We freaked out and grabbed our drugs and our cash and a few things and got in this guy's car. The helicopter followed us for a long time. At some point we ended up at an intersection. We were making a left turn. There just happened to be a car to our left that looked just like ours that was making a left turn at the same time and so it looked like we just went straight. The helicopter followed the other car instead of ours. We decided to leave the state because the cops were getting too close to us.

That night we stayed in a motel in the absolute worst part of town. The room was only $7! It was one of the scariest places I think I have ever been. Everyone left except for Jeff and myself. After about 30 minutes we started hearing lots of people outside the window. They were saying, "I saw those white boys go in that room right there. They look like they had drugs and money. Kick the door in. No just knock first. If they don't answer than we'll break in!" I looked around for something to defend myself with. There was nothing except a chair. I thought about breaking one of the legs off of it and using that to fight, but we were outnumbered 20 to 1. It was frightening to say the least. Jeff and I both thought we were going to die that night. At the moment where they were about to break the door down, one of us finally looked out the window and realized it was just our friends playing a prank on us. I was so happy and so angry all at the same time.

Eventually, we went back to the trailer and settled back in. One night we went to see a concert. It was the Headbanger's Ball Tour of 1989 with Anthrax, Helloween, and Armored Saint. I waited almost a week to trip acid for that show. I wanted it to be good. I ate orange juice concentrate all day long to enhance the trip. I was high as a kite by the time I got there. I dropped 5 hits of acid that night. I made it through the first two bands before I started peaking. During the beginning of Anthrax's set I was laughing and frying my brain hardcore.

Then it happened, the pivotal point of my life had arrived.

I fell back in my chair and I couldn't move for a long time. I started to panic, but still I couldn't move. After what seemed like an eternity I sat up and looked back at my seat. I looked back at my seat only to see myself still in it! I freaked out! I quickly put my hands on my eyes to hide from the horror of it all, but when I did my left eye jumped out of my head and began to twitch around in my hand. I shoved my eye back in my skull and ran my fingers through my hair towards the back of my head. When I did my ears twisted inside my head and disappeared. They made this awful sucking noise that was horrifying. I felt a big flap in the back of my head that I reached my hand into. I was more than a little scared at this point!

I looked around and I wasn't at a concert anymore. I didn't know where I was, but it felt like hell to me. But that couldn't be. I didn't even believe in hell! I was only sixteen years old. I couldn't die yet! I looked for my friends, but they were all gone. In their place were demons, haunting me. They were flying around and taunting me. The things I saw were indescribable! My body started falling apart. Limbs were falling off and the pain was torturous. I realized that hell wasn't just a myth or a fable, it was a real place...and I was there! In an instant, I remembered all the things that I had done wrong. And then they started happening back to me, but worse. All the cruel, heartless things that I had done to people were coming back full circle to where they started. The very ones who tempted me became the same ones who accused me. The lyrics of the bands I worshipped came back to me. The demonic, hateful, murderous lyrics ran through my mind and then they happened to me.

At that point I realized I had died and gone to hell! I was only sixteen years old and my life was over, forever! I would never sleep again. I would never smile again. I would never see a friend again. I would never again have a pleasant experience. Not now, not ever. In a million years I would still be in this rotten place…that I deserved to be in, a place that I had earned and asked for in everything that I did and didn't do.

Who can save you from hell? Who can you go to for help? You can't just take a cold shower, or drink some coffee, or get some sleep and come down. What doctor can make it right? What person can make it right? What could I do to get out of here? I didn't want to be here forever, or at all for that matter!

I tried to think clearly for a moment. I could have just had a bad trip. That happens. So, if that is it then I have to go through this for a lot of hours still. I didn't think I could survive that long. I figured that I would probably kill myself unintentionally. The second option was that I had done too much acid and I was on a permanent trip. In this case I would never come down. There could be flowers and blue skies all around me, but I wouldn't see that because in my mind I would be in hell. In that case I might as well be in hell because I wouldn't know the difference anyway. Then the words came back to me " Acid is dangerous! It is made with strychnine, which is rat poison. You take more than two hits and it could kill you." And that was my third choice… I really was dead and I really was in hell!

There had to be a way out! I vowed to myself that if I had to spend the next thousand years digging my way out of here that I would. I wanted out and I never wanted to come back. I wouldn't wish hell upon my worst enemy! I scrambled in my mind to no avail. There was literally nothing I could do to get out. But then I thought UNLESS there really is a God. He is the only one that could save me from this. There is no one else. There is no other way. I can't get out on my own. For the first time in my life I acknowledged that I couldn't do it on my own. For the first time I humbled myself.

And for the first time I cried out to God, I mean really cried out to God. All I could say was " God, I don't know if you are real. I know I am evil. There is nothing good in me. I know I don't deserve anything from you ...at all. But, you are the only one that can help me. You are my only hope. Please! If you save me from this place I promise I will do anything you ask of me. I will do anything. Please! God! Please save me from this place! Please! Please, save me, Please! I'll do anything! Please! I don't want to be here! I know I deserve all this, but please save me and I will do anything for you! Anything! Please, save me!"

This went on for a few minutes and then I opened my eyes and it was all gone! I had either come back to life or sobered up. Whatever it was I was back! God heard my cry and He saved me!

He brought me back to life! God gave me a second chance!

I saw my friends and told them we had to leave. They must have been really high because they agreed to leave right in the middle of the show.

I told them all about what happened. They were completely unmoved. They said I had a bad trip and that I should trip again as soon as possible so I could get over the bad experience. I was floored at how they just blew the whole thing off as if it was nothing. That night something happened in me. That night was the first time I believed in God. In some cultures I had heard that if you save a man's life than he is your slave for the rest of his life. That is how I felt. Not like I had to, but that I wanted to show my gratitude by a lifetime of service. That was only the beginning, though. I still had a very long road to travel.

4 The Spirit is Willing, but …

Nothing was ever the same for me after that night. Everything was different. I told everyone I knew about how God had saved me from hell. Almost nobody cared. I slowed down on the drug use, but I was still using pretty heavily. I had flashbacks everyday. They were a lot worse when I got high. I had nightmares every night, bad ones. In my dreams I was always fighting demons and darkness. I was always running and afraid. The things I saw were horrifying. I felt like my eyes were bleeding all the time. I couldn't look in the mirror because I was afraid of what I saw. My mind was a mess. It was a sewer of filthy, sinful thoughts and deeds that haunted me every day.

My friends finally wore me down and so I did acid again. It was only one hit, but it was a one way ticket right back to hell. I had to lock myself in my bedroom so that I wouldn't hurt myself or someone else. I thought I would die for sure that night. I was terrified. As soon as it hit me I knew I had messed up in a big way. I cried out to God again, but this time there was no easy way out. The things that happened to me that night were hard to suffer through.

At one point it was as if I saw God come down to me. He was beautiful. He was sparkling and full of colors. He flew down to me with his long flowing beard. He flew right into my face, looked me in the eye, and said, "Now, I have to teach you a lesson!" And then he flew away just as quickly as he came. His colors and his sparkle and his beauty left a trail behind him, but then it started to fade and fall. It turned to ash and fell on me. I looked around me and I was waist deep in sewage! I cried out! I begged for mercy, but there was none to be found. I had broken my promise! I had lied to God! And now I had to pay the price! I somehow made it through the night. I never did acid again and I never want to.

My mother had moved to North Carolina. Since I was a runaway and a dropout I hadn't told her where I was. I could have lost touch with my family completely, but fortunately River gave me her number and address right before they moved.

At some point I made the decision to stop doing drugs. I called my mother and told her that I had quit. The truth is that I had just gotten high (I was probably high at the time actually), but I had made the decision to quit and so for whatever reason I told her. I thought it would make her happy, but I didn't realize it would make her **that** happy. As soon as the words left my lips I knew I had made a mistake. I wasn't really all that serious. It just sounded good at the time. She was ecstatic! Normally, it wouldn't bother me to lie to my mother or anyone else for that matter, but it really bothered me. Somewhere in all this I had started to get my conscience back. She hung up, and I got high again...for the last time. I felt so bad that I had lied to my mother and I had lied to God. I knew that I didn't have many more chances so I quit right then and there.

Somehow I justified the fact that I still sold drugs, because I wasn't using them. After all it was how I made my living. So, I kept selling drugs for another month or so. Because I wasn't high all the time I decided to clean the filthy mess that we all called home. It was disgusting! We would have groups of people sharing needles in the living room. When they were done with the needles they would throw them at the walls like darts. Blood would drip out of the needles down the walls. There were gallon milk jugs full of dip spit, cigarette butts, needles, and every other vile thing you can imagine! You had to actually wade through this place. Nobody ever cleaned and it had been a nonstop party for months. So I cleaned and I cleaned and I cleaned. As I was cleaning I found a small Gideon Bible in Jane's army jacket. I picked it up and something amazing happened. Whatever I had been thinking about just a moment before was exactly what was on the pages as I read the Bible. I read for a while and finally put it down.

Later, I found it again and the same thing happened. I always thought that the Bible was boring useless information for people who were afraid to do anything fun. But, when I picked it up and read it all the answers to life seemed to be in there. I couldn't put it down. I read the whole New Testament and Psalms and Proverbs. I couldn't shut up about what I was reading. It turns out that one of the guys who was living with us, Lee, knew quite a bit about the Bible. I talked to him a lot about the book of Revelation. He showed me how a lot of the prophesies had already come true. I was amazed. So I shared everything I heard with all my friends. More amazing than the prophecies coming true was the fact that most of my friends already knew about them and still chose to live the way that they did. Most of them knew a lot more than I did! How can you know better and still choose to do wrong? It didn't make any sense to me at all!

I started to question everything I was doing. By this time our trailer was a sin circus. We had junkies living with us. Everyone was on meth and all of us had done crack several times. We started to turn on each other. There was a baby in the house who everyone regularly got high just so he would be quiet. We got our dog high all the time too. We had so much stolen stuff in the house it was ridiculous. Duke, another roommate of ours was trading drugs for sex all the time. It was a mess, and for the first time I saw it for what it was. There comes a point in your life where you stop and look back and you say to yourself "What have I become?" Nobody ever says " I want to be a junkie when I grow up." It sneaks up on you. The devil will take you from the whitest white through all the shades of grey so slowly that you don't even notice that you are in the darkest blackness by the end of the whole thing.

Russell and Duke were getting out of control so Lee and Jane and I decided to kick them out of the trailer since it was in Jane's name. They refused to leave; so one night when they were out we put all their stuff out on the porch with a note on it. They didn't like that at all! They smashed Lee's car beyond recognition while we watched from inside. They slashed all his tires and broke all the glass and dented everything that could be dented. Lee loved his car. He had gotten it because of a medical injury. Then they kicked the front door in. Russell stood up on our coffee table, stomped on my Bible, and shoved a sawed off shotgun in my face (some junkie had stolen a police riot shotgun from a cop and sawed off the end of it. He traded it to us for dope.)

Russell almost killed me that night. They took everything in the house. They vandalized everything in the house. When they finally left we called 911. The cops wouldn't do anything at all to help us. Russell and Duke came back six times and did the same thing. We called 911 every time. The fastest the cops ever got there was six hours. Most of the time they never came at all. We told them where Russell and Duke were staying, their names, what had happened, and many other details that they would need to take care of the situation. The cops wouldn't do anything, even with a baby there they wouldn't do anything to help. I'm sure they knew who and what we were. I'm sure they thought they were going to let the scum kill itself or something like that.

Well, since the cops wouldn't help us, Jeff stole his dad's gun. One day we were driving when Russell and Duke pulled up behind us. I got the gun out, loaded it, and got ready to kill them both. We pulled over. By the grace of God, they drove on. I never killed anyone, but that day I would have killed my best friends and I know they would have killed me. I am so thankful that they didn't stop.

Shortly after that I was staying the night at Jeff's house. He passed out around eleven or so, but I had quit doing drugs and drinking so I was still ready to stay up until dawn. I remember feeling like I was literally in heaven because Jeff had a clean shower and real food at his house. It was so wonderful! Jeff had a little brother who was my age named Damion. Damion was a Christian and I had always made fun of him for it. I made fun of all the church kids. Someone had a shirt that said "Love God, Hate Sin". I used to mix it up and say "Love Sin, Hate God". I was always really mean to Damion. He didn't do anything that the cool people did. He was a virgin who didn't smoke, drink, cuss, or do drugs. And I let him know how stupid he was for all that.

Jeff had passed out in the other room and I was bored. I went out to the living room and there was Damion watching the Prayer Channel at eleven o' clock on a Friday night. All I could think was "man, you are the nerd that the nerds make fun of. You have got to be the biggest loser there is." But I was so bored that I sat down on the floor and watched it too.

The pastor on this show might as well have been talking to me. He called out my life and didn't miss a note. He preached on the book of Revelation and spoke of how I needed to repent while there was still time. Then he said "if anyone listening right now needs something from God than pray with me right now."

I wanted so badly to pray with that pastor that night. I wanted so badly to have God hear my voice and for him to heal me, but I didn't know how to pray. And I knew that I was worthless. I knew that I had nothing to give to God. I could tell you all about the depths of hell, but I couldn't think of one good thing. NOT EVEN ONE!

I was lost and there was absolutely no hope for me at all. I had escaped hell once, but let's face it... I would go back, eventually. That was where I belonged. That was what I deserved and it was all I knew. Oh, how I wished that I could be good, that I could somehow make up for all the rottenness and evil in me. But I knew I could never do enough good to make up for all the bad things I had done. My heart was broken. I started crying. I didn't make a scene or anything, I just quietly cried. The show ended and I think Damion figured out that I had been crying.

He asked me what was wrong. I thought, "Ok, here it comes. He is going to kick me while I'm down. All those times I have been mean to him are about to come back to me. I guess I deserve it. Just take it like a man, John." Instead something amazing happened. Damion actually cared what about was wrong with me. How could he? After the way I had treated him, how could he want to do anything but hurt me? I was touched, truly touched.

He asked what was the matter and I told him that I was trying to get my life cleaned up, but I didn't think I could ever make up for all the bad things I had done. He opened up his Bible and showed me all kinds of things. He told me that I was right about not being able to make up for the evil I had done. I never could. So, Jesus came down and paid the price for me. He made it right, because I couldn't. He took my punishment, just because he loved me...and he would have done it if I was the only person who needed saving! All I could think was "Why would anyone do that for me? Don't you know what I am? I am worthless." I told him that he didn't understand. I was a lot worse than the average person. He told me about the people whom Jesus chose to be his disciples: the tax collectors, the thieves, the prostitutes, the drunks, and the sinners. **He came to heal that which was broken**, and I fell into that category in the worst way.

Then he asked me what I thought heaven was like. I had never really given it any thought. I figured it was boring and empty. That there were angels floating around singing lame music and playing harps and stuff. That was about it. I guess they did good stuff, since only really good people went there. I didn't know. I could tell him about hell if he wanted to know. He listened to me ramble for a while. Then, he opened up Revelation: Chapter 21 and 22 and read to me.

" Then I saw a new heaven and a new earth, for the first heaven and the first earth had passed away, and there was no longer any sea. I saw the Holy City, the New Jerusalem, coming down out of heaven from God, prepared as a bride beautifully dressed for her husband. And I heard a loud voice from the throne saying 'Now the dwelling of God is with men, and he will live with them. They will be his people and he will be their God. He will wipe away every tear from their eyes. There will be no more death or mourning or crying or pain, for the old order of things has passed away." It goes on to talk about streets made of gold so pure that it is like transparent glass. It talks of walls of jewels and precious stones of every kind. It speaks of gates made of pearls. It talks of absolute perfection, but a few things were enough for me: No more tears or pain or death and we will see God face to face. That is enough for me. If heaven is a dumpster with no more pain, no more tears, no more death, and no more sorrow than sign me up. The fact that it is so much more is only a bonus for me.

But then Damion showed me other scriptures that said "No eye has seen, no ear has heard, nor has it even entered into the mind of man what God has in store for those that love him." So Damion asked me what the most beautiful things I had seen and heard and imagined were. I listed a few things and then it dawned on me it is nothing compared to heaven! And then I saw the beauty of it all for the first time. Heaven wasn't a boring, drab place. It was everything great you could ever imagine imagining and more! I was excited for a minute and then I remembered that heaven was a place that I could never, ever hope to be. I wanted it more than you could imagine, but I knew I wasn't good enough. I shouldn't even hope for such a thing.

Damion, talked to me for a long time and finally he asked if I wanted to pray. I wanted to so badly, but I told him I didn't know how. He said just to repeat after him, so I did. **"Jesus, I know that I am a sinner. I know that you paid the price for my sins. Please forgive me. I believe in you."** I'm sure it was a disgrace of a prayer from a disgrace of a person if you were to ask any "church person", but it was the most amazing thing that had ever happened to me! Once again God met me where I was! I know he heard my prayer and I know he forgave me, even though I didn't know why he would. I was never the same again. Everyone I knew said that I was the biggest "night and day conversion" that they had ever seen. I don't think Damion ever knew what a difference he made in my life. Thank you so much for letting Christ shine through you, Damion Patino! You have no idea what you did for me. You changed my life forever and gave me hope when I had none. Thank you!

Time passed. I was talking so much about the Bible all the time that Lee invited me to his parent's church. I thought that lightning would strike me if I got near a church, so I told him no. I was willing to accept God's gift but still wouldn't come to His house because I was ashamed and ignorant. I didn't understand that church is a hospital for sinners not a museum for saints. He tried all kinds of ways to persuade me, but I had a great excuse every time. Until he told me they were having a barbecue...a FREE BBQ! It had been such a long time since I had had any real food that I couldn't say no. So, we went.

It was a long drive. I don't even know where we went. We drove with the T-Tops down the whole way there. We showed up 45 minutes late, I was wearing an Iron Maiden T-shirt, I had long hair that was a mess from the wind, I was barefoot, I didn't know anyone, I was strung-out looking, and Lee started walking in the church. I stopped him and said, "Have you looked at us? We can't go in there!" He insisted that we had come all this way and we weren't going to stop now, so we went in. I thought we could just slip in the back unnoticed and then eat afterwards. Well, there were only about 10 pews in the whole church and when we opened the door everyone knew. They all turned around and looked at us, and I thought, "Here it comes."

There was an awkward pause for a moment and then the pastor stopped everything. He waved us to the front and welcomed us in. With a smile he said "Come on in, have a seat. Let me tell you what we have been talking about today." I was like, "Well, ok." So, he rewinds and briefs us on his entire sermon. He talked about Revelation as well. He also asked if anyone wanted to pray and ask God for something. He told a story about a boy in their town. He said, " I had a boy come into church who I knew was a trouble-maker. I hadn't seen him in church for a long time, but I figured he would be back next week when I had planned on giving a sermon spelling out the salvation message. I would tell him then. I let the boy go without the message I should have told him. That week they found him dead in a stock tank. I will never again pass up an opportunity to share the gospel. NOW is the appointed time! Today is the day of salvation!"

I wanted to go up and pray so bad it hurt, but I had a lot of marks against me so I stayed in my seat. Lee kept elbowing me and finally I got the courage to stand up and take a step forward. The pastor asked me "What can I do for you young man?" I said, "Well, I think I want to be baptized." He asked why and I started crying uncontrollably and said, "Because I'm a sinner." We prayed. When we were done he turned me around to the congregation and he said "All the angels in heaven rejoice when even one sinner comes to repentance and I can hear them rejoicing for John today! Come up here and welcome him into the family of God."

They lined up single file and one by one hugged me and shook my hand and gave me some words of encouragement. I had never seen anything like it! Were they blind? Did they not see the miserable wretch that stood before them? I wasn't something to rejoice over, I was something to run from. But for whatever reason they just loved me, and that was that. And then they fed me. It was delicious!

Later that day I talked to Lee's mother. She had a tumor in her eye that was making her go blind and was going to kill her soon. She wasn't afraid or bitter or upset. She truly had hope. I could see it in her. She had no fear at all. She wasn't afraid to die, and she didn't feel cheated about losing her sight. She inspired me. I had never seen that before in my life. Never!

We arranged for me to be baptized the next Sunday. My mother flew down from North Carolina to watch me get baptized and so did the rest of my family. It was in a small stock tank, which is like a small lake. There were stickers (porcupine eggs) all over the place and it looked like there could be snakes in the water, but I didn't care. I got in the water with the pastor and his helper. I felt dirty with sin. He said "John Tunnell, I now baptize you in the name of the Father and the Son and the Holy Spirit." He dipped me in the water and when I came out of the water I felt like the sin stayed in the water, but I left. I felt clean for the first time in my life. On July 29, 1989 the old me died once and for all, and I became a new creation! Hallelujah!

Everything looked different to me. It was like my eyes had been opened. The world just looked different. It was like being born all over, like being born again! I guess that is why they call us "Born Again Christians." Mock if you like, but I have never been the same since. I was a wretched hopeless individual, but no more! Now, I was a child of God and I was forgiven! Hallelujah! Do you know what that feels like? It is amazing! If you think acid is hard to describe to someone who has never done it, try explaining the feeling of salvation to someone who has never experienced it. It is like trying to explain colors to a blind man. They have no point of reference. Nothing to compare to that you can describe.

My Baptism July 29ᵗʰ, 1989

Do you know why we have middle names? It is interesting. Of course thousands of years ago people just had a single name, Adam for example. Everyone knew Adam. After all, there was only one of him. Once there were more people then you had to identify a specific Adam by calling him Adam the blacksmith. Over time that simply became Adam Smith. Since most fathers passed their trade on to their son they just kept the same last name. Women didn't necessarily have trades so they took their husband's last name. But middle names didn't come along until later.

When someone became a Christian, when they met Jesus, they felt so much like a different person that their old name didn't even apply anymore. The old man had died and the new man they had become deserved a new name. So Saul became Paul, Simon became Peter, and so on. This was known as their "Christian" name, and still is to this day. These were really only given to people who had been born again.

However, over time the Catholic Church did what organized religion has done since the beginning. They wanted to cover all their bases so they started baptizing babies when they were born and giving them Christian names straight out of the womb. So, instead of Simon waiting to meet Jesus and then becoming Peter he would just be born Simon Peter whatever his last name was, "Fisherman" maybe.

The point is that when you are truly changed, when you meet Jesus and he saves your soul, when there isn't a shadow of doubt that he is real and he loves you and he paid the price for you, then it changes everything about you forever! Hallelujah for that! I have been redeemed! I have been saved! To all the people in my life who have mocked in ignorance asking, "what I have been saved from exactly" now you know. I have been saved from myself. I have been saved from sin. I have been saved from death and hell. I have been saved from more than I can ever explain or even know. I don't understand all the intimate details of the process of digestion, but that doesn't stop me from eating. I don't understand all the intimate details of salvation either, but this I do know I was dead and now I am alive! I was blind, but now I see!

If you are called to be a witness in court you don't have to know everything about the case. You don't have to decide who is guilty or who is innocent. You don't even have to be familiar with the law. You simply answer the questions asked of you and tell what you saw and what you heard. So, as a witness for God that is all I am doing is telling you what I saw and what I heard. Could it all have been in my mind or just a coincidence? Maybe? However, I think what determines a miracle is that you asked and you received... the impossible. But more importantly you just **know** that God heard you and He answered you. He took the time to hear my cry and to save me, expecting nothing in return. I will never be the same!

We all celebrated my baptism that day. My family was there, some friends, and a lot of strangers. I never went back to that church again. I don't remember the name of it, the pastor, or even the town it was in. I wish I could remember so I could go back and thank those people for loving a broken boy in trouble. I don't know if they feel as if they failed because they didn't keep up with me, but if any of you ever read this I want you to know you gave me enough inspiration to last a lifetime. Thank you!

I felt like I had gone out on my own and found God, or he found me. Either way, I did it alone. That couldn't have been farther from the truth. That is NEVER the case! If you stagger back home it is only by the grace of God and an awful lot of prayer from people who love you. What a beautiful, beautiful thing! It turns out that my mother had started going to a Bible study and had been praying for me for a long time. Not just her, but the whole group. Not just them, as years go by I meet people from my past that tell me how amazed they are that I have changed. Then they tell me how much they used to pray for me. To those of you who feel discouraged about your prayers, don't be discouraged. God hears... and he answers. In His time, and His timing is perfect. Thank you to all of you who have prayed for me through the years. I hope one day you know what a difference you made in my life.

5   The Pearl Of Great Price

"The kingdom of heaven is like treasure hidden in a field. When a man found it, he hid it again, and then in his joy went and sold all he had and bought that field"

- *Matthew 13:44*

As I was saying everyone referred to my conversion as the biggest night and day change they had ever seen. I didn't see what the big deal was. I just figured everyone didn't know the truth and so they hadn't changed because they didn't know, so I would tell them. It was that simple. I didn't know, now I do, so I changed, you can too. I am, of course, an idiot! Most people do know the truth and they refuse to make the change. Why? I'll never know. It doesn't make sense to me at all. I wasn't going to let that stop me. Surely there are those who just need a little inspiring, a little knowledge, a little love, and they will change. And for those I will keep trying. How can you shut up about something so amazing? I couldn't then and I can't now. I am so lucky and so blessed, but you can be too. **What are you waiting for?**

Well, I didn't shut up. I talked about Jesus to everyone I met. At first I was a little shy, but then I read where Jesus said *"Whoever acknowledges me before others, I will also acknowledge before my Father in heaven. But whoever disowns me before others, I will disown before my Father in heaven." – Matt. 10: 32-33.* And I read where Paul said, *"For I am not ashamed of the gospel, because it is the power of God that brings salvation to everyone who believes." – Romans 1:16.* I would rather be a fool in the eyes of men, than a fool in the eyes of God. I didn't want to be denied by Jesus and I certainly wasn't ashamed so I didn't close my mouth to anyone. If the Bible said it, then it was true. If God asked me to do it, then I would. End of discussion. It wasn't a question. The only question was what exactly does God want ME to do?

As you can imagine my drug friends quickly got tired of me. I thought we were friends, and the drugs were secondary. It turns out our only common interest was the drugs. Once I quit using they didn't want me around anymore. It was a little hurtful. I'll have to admit. I was ready to leave anyway. So, in August of 1989 I flew back to live with my family in North Carolina for a while. In the airport in Dallas I saw a guy named James with a guitar. I went up and talked to him. I've never really been shy. We ended up talking in the airport and on the plane. We became good friends and still see each other 28 years later. It turns out that he lived a few minutes from where my mother lived. He seemed very interested in what I had to say about God and my experiences.

I spent the next few months detoxing. I went cold turkey off of everything. It was hard. I had headaches. I had withdrawals. I had flashbacks and nightmares. Terrible nightmares. I had the shakes. It was a hard time. I used the time I had to read the whole Bible, Old and New Testaments. My body wanted to get high, but I wouldn't do it. It was probably easier because I was in a new state and I didn't have connections.

I know I could have found them if I had wanted to, but instead I used the opportunity to stay away from drugs. I cut all my hair off. It had gotten pretty long again. One of the main reasons I quit getting high, besides the terrible flashbacks, was that I felt very strongly that the rapture would happen any minute. I felt like we were in the end times and it was very, very close. I didn't want to be high and have to stand before God to give an account of my life and be too high to give a straight answer. Sounds dumb, I know. Either way, it helped me quit.

So, whatever my lame reason was to quit. I did. The only way to do it and to do it right is to put it down and never even consider picking it back up again. You walk away and you never look back, never! So, I never did. No matter how bad it hurt or how bad I wanted it, I never did it again. If I can do it, you can too. Any excuse you have to not quit is just that, an excuse to not quit. If you want to, you will. The end. No excuses.

Once I had gotten over the worst of the withdrawals I started realizing that there was a lot more wrong with my life than just drugs. I was a mess. I read in James where it says how can salt water and fresh water come from the same spring? It is impossible! With the same mouth you praise God and you curse men. I realized that I preached all the time, but still had a potty mouth. I didn't mean to, it was just habit. Well then, it was a habit that I had to break. So I did. I used substitute cuss words instead of real ones and after a while I got used to it. Darn it. I felt the same way about cussing as I did about drugs. You have to put it down and never pick it up again. So, I did. I walked away, forever. No matter what happened I determined within myself to never cuss again, and I haven't. At the time I am writing this it has been 28 years with no alcohol, no tobacco, no drugs, and no cussing. Not by my own strength, but by the grace of God.

In AA and NA they tell you that you are always an addict. For the rest of your life they say you are an addict. Part of me believes that. The fact that I know that I could fall again if I let myself slip keeps me from falling. I know that I have it in me to do terrible things, so I refuse to do them. I know what the far end of that road looks like and what it leads to. I am not interested in going there again, so I keep myself in check. God will never give you more than you can bear, and when we are tempted there will always be a way of escape. And no temptation has fallen you except that which is common to man. If God says it then it is true. So, I believe. When I am tempted, which is every single day, I look for the way of escape and it is always there. It isn't easy, but it is there. Every time you say yes it gets easier and easier to say yes. No matter what the situation. And every time you say no it gets easier and easier to say no. So, I started saying no, and now it comes without a second thought. At first it took everything I had, now I laugh if someone offers me drugs. Not only do I laugh, everyone around me laughs.

After I conquered all those things I realized that the music that I listened to wasn't helping me either. It was a hard decision, but I sorted through my music and destroyed about $5,000 worth of posters, tapes, tapestries, T-shirts, mirrors, autographed items, CD's, etc. I know you might be thinking why didn't you sell it? You could have made so much money! I know. I thought about that too. I couldn't pass on the curse that had almost killed me, so I took the loss and destroyed all of it. That was hard to do. I loved that music. I held some stuff back that wasn't that bad, but after a few weeks I threw that away too.

I loved playing the guitar! Loved it! All I knew how to play was satanic music though, so I tried to make up good music. I couldn't. I wrestled with this one for a while, but I finally decided to give away my guitars, amps, effects, and everything. I doubted I would ever get to play again, and it broke my heart. I guess I figured that if God wanted me to play the guitar that maybe I could play when I got to heaven. The point was that I wasn't going to have anything stand between God and I, and I wasn't going to keep something around that was killing me. So, I gave it away. Wow! That hurt! I can't tell you how bad it hurt.

Then there were the dreams and the flashbacks. I had gotten so used to them that I didn't really think there was any hope of changing them. I had nightmares EVERY night! I'll give you just a few examples. One night I woke up in my room alone. Everything was where it should have been. I knew I wasn't sleeping. I laid there in the still of the night for a moment and then I felt a heavy darkness fill the room. It was all around me and on top of me, but not in me. All of the sudden I couldn't move or speak! I couldn't cry out! I was paralyzed. I was terrified...again. It was as if a demon had come back to haunt me. I could feel it in my face. I could feel it breathing. I knew that if I could just breathe the name of Jesus that he would have to leave because the Bible says that if you resist the devil he must flee. But I couldn't speak. I laid there frozen in fear struggling to speak for about 10 minutes until I finally squeezed it out: "Jesus please help me." And then the darkness left in an instant. The room was quiet and peaceful. The name of Jesus is powerful. Demons run at the mention of his name. Believe me, I know.

Another time I had a demon chasing me all night long. It was trying to kill me with a huge sword. It always seemed to be just a step behind me, but as hard as I ran I couldn't gain any ground. He was always right there on me. I paced myself and learned to run with longer paces so that I would still run as fast and as far, but I wouldn't have to move my legs as much. I ran all night long, and I don't remember if I ever turned around to face my fear. I may have just kept running. I was exhausted when I woke up, but then again I always was.

I had lots of dreams about going back to hell. They were graphic and disturbing. I finally talked to someone about it and they asked if I had prayed about it yet. I had never even considered praying about it. The thought never even crossed my mind. I figured I was legally insane anyway after all the acid and so I would just have to live with it for the rest of my life. But then he told me about a scripture that said God had given us over to a sound mind. So, I believed and I prayed about it and I never had another nightmare. Praise God, he answers prayers!

I did have another dream though. I was asleep in my room. Once again, I woke up and everything was where it should have been. I was definitely awake. I laid there in the stillness for a little while. Then the room lit up like the morning sun, even though it was night still. I looked out my window and there was a cloud right in front of my window. Everything else had fallen away except my room and this cloud outside my window. On the cloud stood three men. The one in the middle was brilliant. I couldn't see his face because it shone like the sun, but I knew it was Jesus. On either side of him there were two black men in robes and I knew they were angels. I thought it was interesting that they were black men. I felt like it was their reward for having to put up with all the racism and hatred and slavery all those years. They looked at me and called me out of my room because it was time to go home. So, I stepped out with them and we rose up to heaven. Of course I woke up before I ever got there, but I will never forget the amazing peace I felt or the incredible joy to finally be going home! I didn't give a second thought to anything I was leaving behind; it was nothing in comparison to what was ahead. I think that is the first good dream I can ever remember. I will never forget it.

So, I had successfully cleaned up my life in a relatively short amount of time. I had taken my own advice. I had taken the plank out of my own eye so I could see clearly the speck in another's. What a humbling experience. You should try it sometime. It will make you a lot more understanding of other people's shortcomings. It will give you mercy and compassion and love for others because you know how hard it is to conquer something that has you in a death grip. But it can be done. Hallelujah, it can be done!

I got sick of sitting around doing nothing. I thought the rapture would have happened by now. I still figured it would come any minute. The Amish have a saying "**Live each day as if Jesus died last week, rose yesterday, and is coming back today. But work like he won't be back for a thousand years.**" I wanted to be the guy that when my master came back he found me doing what He had asked, so I tried. I heard Billy Graham say that no man deserves to hear the gospel twice while another man hasn't heard it at all. That hit home to me. So, I tried to be a missionary.

I tried every place that I could find and always got the same response. "Kid, go back to school and get your diploma first, then go to college, then seminary, then do some kind of specialized training, and then if you still want to go we'll put you on a waiting list." There wasn't time for all that! And why do you want to educate the fire out of me anyway? I have a desire, a need to tell people about Jesus. Send me! I am willing. Send me! Please, someone send me! Finally, someone sent me. One of my mother's friends from the Bible study that had prayed for me to get saved was a friend with someone at Jesus People, USA in Chicago. He talked to his friend and they said I could come. I saw the ad for it in a magazine. It said, "Can you fit everything you have in one bag? Yes, you can!" It said more than that, but that was part of it.

I gave away everything else I had and I went. First I flew back to Texas to stay with Bill for a week. He encouraged me a lot to be a better Christian. It seemed like everyone I met was helping me to be a better Christian. He painted houses for a living. So, for a week or so I did too. I learned a lot. One of the first things I learned was that 5 AM really existed. I had heard of 5 AM before and I had seen it from the getting ready for bed side of things, but who wanted to get up that early? The answer. Bill did, and apparently so did I. I had him send all the money I made that week to my mother. I figured she deserved it and I didn't really want any money.

So, the week ended and I got on the plane to Chicago. Deep down, I really felt like it was a test just to see if I would really go. To see if I really would give everything up and leave everything I knew to follow God. Once he saw that I really would do it I could just go home. God had a different plan for me. I got to Jesus People, USA in September of 1989. It was cold. The people were really nice. We walked down the streets to the homeless shelter where I would be living. They were lined with homeless people, pathetic, hopeless looking ones. How does this happen? How do you let yourself get this low? (As if that wasn't the pot calling the kettle black. Look where I had just come from!) I saw more homeless people in any one day in Chicago, than I have in the rest of my life combined. It was staggering. It was total culture shock. I kept thinking if you are going to be homeless and in poverty anyway why not go somewhere warmer? The wind chill got down to eighty degrees below zero. That's COLD! Start walking south!!! At least you won't freeze to death!

I stayed in a small room with 5 or 8 guys. I, of course, seemed to be the only one who actually believed the line about fitting all your belongings in just one bag. Everyone else had tons of stuff. Oh well. They were all very nice and encouraging. I worked in the kitchen. I cleaned, mopped, washed dishes, cooked, served the homeless people, cleaned the bathrooms, and whatever else needed to be done. It was hard work. I thought it would be a little more glamorous, but it was fulfilling. I was actually doing something constructive with my life and I was helping people. I got put on a roofing crew. I want to interject here and say that roofing is one of the hardest jobs out there. You work hard all day. You sweat, you bleed, and you work some more, then you go home and hurt all night long until you wake up and do it again. I learned a lot though, about roofing and about myself.

I spent all my free time in the shelter with the people. I talked with them and listened to them. It was a rough neighborhood. We heard glass breaking and gunshots all the time. People hardly even reacted. It was sad really. There was this guy in a wheelchair named Bernie. He was in his 50's. He had been in a war or two. Like everyone else there he was a little crazy. He told me about all the people he had killed in the war... and since the wars. He told me about people he had murdered in the alleys of Chicago. It was disturbing. I don't know if anyone else listened to him, but I did.

One day he crapped all over himself. He was too embarrassed to tell anyone, but it was obvious. No one wanted to clean him up and he couldn't do it himself because he was in a wheelchair. I was assigned the task. It wasn't fun by any stretch, but I tried to make him feel comfortable about the whole thing. There was a lot of gross stuff I had to do there, but I always thought about the fact that whatsoever you do for the least of these, you do unto me. So, I thought I could do this for Jesus after all he has done for me.

After a few months I got pretty sick. My mother came to visit me. We talked for a while and she said I should come home and we could start our own mission somewhere. I agreed. I left about a week later and went back to North Carolina. If we were going to start our own mission we would need some money, so I found a job.

I was a dishwasher and general maintenance man at Applebee's restaurant. I was making $5 an hour. I worked doubles all the time. I worked as much as possible to save money as quickly as possible. I read up on building a little bit. My mother bought me an acoustic guitar. It was beautiful! I hadn't played guitar in way too long. I didn't know any Christian music so I didn't know what to play. I told God that I would only use my music skills for his glory from that moment on. Amazingly enough I developed quite a talent for song writing. I started writing music all the time. I loved it!

I was a machine at work. I worked more hours than anyone up there. I even got some kind of an award for it! Everyone knew if they didn't want to work that I would pick up their shift for them. I never complained and I never slowed down. I did whatever they asked me to do. They wanted to promote me because I was a good worker, but I told them this was only temporary. I was happy being a dishwasher. I was good at it.

Everyone talked about the fact that I turned down promotions and that I worked like a slave. The Bible said to work as if you are working for the Lord, so I did. There was this one cook who hated me. He used to throw tomatoes at me, and nasty food, and knives. One night he poured bleach all over my feet and made a lot of the skin on my feet peel off. Another night I had opened the store and closed it. It was about two or three in the morning. I had just cleaned the bathrooms again. I was exhausted. I came back into the kitchen and he hosed me down with scalding hot water from head to toe while everyone watched and laughed at me.

Later he asked me "Do you know why I pick on you?" And I said, "Yes, I know." He said, "It's because you are a Christian! And I hate that about you. I used to be a Christian too. Then I got a girl pregnant and got into drugs. The same thing will happen to you. You will fall and I want to watch it. But all you ever say when I pick on you is 'no big deal'. What is the matter with you?" I tried to explain, but he didn't care.

Not long after that I walked into the kitchen and overheard some people talking badly about me. Then I heard the guy that had picked on me stick up for me. Later, he got me alone and he said, "Do you know why I stood up for you?" And I didn't, really. He said, "Because you are a Christian. And you live what you believe. That is rare. I won't let anyone say anything bad about you. You have my respect." I was shocked. What a compliment! What an honor! By the time I left everyone seemed sad to see me go. They offered me more money, but it was never about the money and they knew that. They laughed a little about how I was going off to the wilderness, into the unknown. I had saved $5,000 in six months working for $5 an hour. I had saved almost everything I made. I had sacrificed and worked hard. I was proud of myself.

I took the money and bought a camper/truck. I've never seen anything like it before or since. I got it for $1,800. I didn't have a driver's license yet, but I bought it so my mother could drive us. Once again I sold or gave away everything I had and stepped out in faith. River and Ann didn't share my enthusiasm about stepping out in faith. The day we were supposed to move they both ran away. That wasn't a fun day. The cops got involved. We found them both, put them in the back of the camper and didn't stop for gas until we got to Tennessee. We drove all the way to Washington State in less than four days. I should say my mom drove the camper and I drove my mom...crazy. I kept her awake and kept telling her we could make it just a little longer. We were all slap happy by the end of the trip.

We looked at a few pieces of property and then found one we bought on the spot in Republic. Which is about 30 miles south of Grand Forks, Canada and 3 hours North of Spokane, WA. We got 20 acres of land for $16,000. It was zero down and zero interest and only $159 a month. It took two days to find the land once we got to Washington. We didn't have a clue where we would be going. We just went. That was July 1990. I was 17 years old.

I didn't waste any time. We had needs and limited cash. I bought a shovel and (what I thought was) an axe. I cleared some brush out of the way and dug a pit to have fires in. We cooked over the fire and used it for warmth. There was a park that you could take showers in for less than a dollar, plus we went swimming in the nearby lake to cool off and clean up. We went to the bathroom out in the woods. I put an end to that pretty quick. I dug an outhouse the next day. It took a few days, but I did it. My mom helped with everything. She also kept the peace and kept us fed which wasn't easy out in the woods. River and Ann refused to help at all. Chris was only 5 years old at the time.

After the outhouse was done I started to dig a well. Fortunately for us there was an aspen grove on the property. Aspen trees have shallow roots so that means there is water close to the surface. It was hard digging but I hit water three feet down. After that I went to start cutting down trees to build the log cabin. I had bought an axe because I didn't want to pay $400 for a chainsaw. I could do it by hand. What is the big deal? So, I picked up my splitting maul (that I thought was an axe) and went to it...for hours...on one lousy little tree! I was so exhausted by the time that stupid tree fell that I just went and bought a chainsaw. I'm so glad I didn't know what an axe was at the time. I might have actually tried to cut down all those trees by hand if I thought it was possible.

I knew we had to have a good foundation, but none of the trees looked big enough to use as piers. That night there was a big storm and it blew down the biggest tree on our property, which became our foundation. If there is one thing I have learned in my life it is this: "Where God guides, God provides". He provided a solid foundation for my life and now for my house. We cut the tree up and rolled the pieces towards our building site. We dug holes for the piers, treated the stumps, and buried them. Then we proceeded to cut down more trees, and cut the limbs off of them, and peel the bark off of them, and cut them to length, and roll them over, and lift them up, and notch them like Lincoln logs with a chainsaw, and spike them in place.

We built the roof. We had 5 windows and a door. We had a wood burning stove for heat and cooking. It was mostly one big room 24 feet by 24 feet with a bathroom and a loft. The bathroom was a bathtub with a drain that went right under the house. We had a pitcher pump on the well and we pumped water into buckets. Then we would pour water into this solar sack, which was a black rubber bag with a nozzle on the bottom of it. If you left it outside in the sun the blackness would soak up the heat from the sun. When it got up to temperature we would take turns in the bath. It was pretty archaic, but it worked. Come to think of it, most of the time we would just boil water, mix it with cold water, and put that in the solar sack. It wasn't fun, but we did it.

We were the talk of the town. Republic only has about 1,500 people so you get to know everybody pretty quickly. Everyone talked about the crazy kid and his mom building that cabin up in the woods outside of town. Those people were so nice to us. People would come by everyday and give advice or have something they could do to help. There was a nice couple up the mountain from us. The guy's name was Jersey. He had been a horse vet for racehorses. He would ride his horse down the mountain everyday and see how we were doing. He was about seventy years old. Then there was a family a few miles away that had a ranch. I would do odd jobs for them to get enough money to keep the house project going. I built a corral for them, repaired their fences, and bucked bails of hay (hard work).

People would bring us food all the time. The building inspector became a great friend of ours. He was very helpful and kind. In the middle of the whole thing we had to keep dealing with problems like bears and coyotes... and being ignorant. We also had to deal with River and Ann. Ann ran away several times and kept getting in trouble. Child Protective Services got involved. River moved back to North Carolina to join a band. He dropped out of school and got a job. He was 14 years old when he left home. He did successfully complete the eighth grade before dropping out of school forever.

River ended up as a manager at a steak house within no time. He had the keys and the codes to the store. I guess they didn't know he couldn't even legally work yet. He rode a skateboard to work. It took three hours one way to get to work. His roommate and band mate charged him gas money to give him a ride to work. So, a lot of the time River would sleep in fields or Laundromats or Denny's restaurants so that he wouldn't have to do another skateboard marathon for six hours round trip. If anyone sacrificed them self for music, it is River. He has applied himself more than anyone I have ever met.

So, we finished the log cabin in seven weeks and moved into it in September. It was already getting cold. This guy named Don owned a backhoe service. He came and dug the well out to a respectable depth and filled it with a culvert and gravel and a lid. He also graded our road, which was at least a mile. I had told him that we were poor. When the time came to pay him he wouldn't let me give him more than $500 for all that work. He is one of the many people in my life that didn't claim to be a Christian, but what he did was very Christ-like even if he didn't want anyone to know. To everyone in Republic who helped us, which was almost everyone, thank you.

We needed money so I started doing odd jobs all the time. I did anything I was asked to do. I chopped down trees, split firewood, built anything and everything, picked apples (hard work), and did a lot of construction. I got a job with one of the contractors in town and got to help build a chiropractic clinic and a bank. It was cool. I learned a lot.

The cabin was freezing! A family invited us to stay at their house for a while. There was some great reason at the time. Whatever it was, their house was warm. We had been going to the Catholic Church in town and met them there. I actually ended up helping build an addition to the church fellowship hall at that church.

Jamie, the oldest son of the family we were staying with, invited me to the Church of the Nazarene. I liked it a lot! Everyone was nice and the preaching was right on with the Bible. That was the first church I was ever a member of. I got really involved. I helped out wherever I could. I kept doing construction through the winter. I learned a lot about building. Building is very interesting. There are a lot of lessons in life if you pay attention. In fact if you pay attention, there are lessons all around us. All you have to do is look.

One of the cool things about God is that He speaks to each of us in our own language. Not just English or Spanish or French, but individually. There are things that would take lots of time to explain to a stranger that I already know because of my life experience. Instead of picking some obscure thing that I don't understand God looks at something I am familiar with and says, "See it's like this. Do you get it?" He does the same thing to you. Are you listening?

Over the winter I started wondering where the mission part of our journey had gone. It was nice to have work and have a place to stay, but I wanted to do something more with my life. It wasn't like I was doing nothing. I just wanted to do more. I struggled with what I should do. My mom is always wise. I am always spontaneous and rash. Sometimes she sees clearly when I don't. I was talking to her one night and trying to figure out what I could do with my life. She said I should go finish school and try to be a pastor. She said "The only time you are truly happy is when you are sharing the gospel with someone. John, go and do that."

I had already dropped out, two years before. I was so far behind that I could never catch up, or so I thought. There is something empowering about having someone you know believe in you. She told me that I was smart and I could do anything I set my mind to. She said she believed in me. So, I went and took my GED. I aced it. It was easy. I made up for two and half years of high school in a few hours. The next challenge was how to get into a college and then how to pay for it! You can't study to be a pastor at a state school, so you have to go to a private school. Northwest Nazarene College is the one everyone said I should go to. It was $10,000 a year.

There was a lady at the church named Phyllis Mason. Phyllis truly is a woman of God. She was a single mom with two teenagers my age. She worked at the community college for $8 an hour. She helped everyone she knew. It was unbelievable that one woman could have such an impact on a community. Even though she didn't have much she never complained about it. She helped out at the church all the time. She played piano several times a week for services. She let the youth groups and Sunday school classes meet in her house. She shared everything she had... without reservation. The way she figured God gave her everything she had, and he gave it to her to share not to be hoarded.

If anyone needed a ride she would give it. If someone was hungry she would feed them. Anyone who needed a place to stay could stay at her place. She visited people in prison all the time. She stretched herself beyond her comfort zone all the time. She said, "God gives blessings to those that God can give blessings through." If you needed an ear to hear your problems she was there for you. She could quote the Bible, but she also actually applied it to her life. Lots of people can quote the Bible, but not many actually apply it to their life. She lived a holy life. Nobody could say anything bad about her. And she was the only person I believe when she said "I will pray for you." The woman is a prayer warrior. I am not. I am a terrible pray-er. Phyllis on the other hand still tells me that she prays for me every day, and like I said, I actually believe her.

Anyway, she worked at the college and she helped me get my college application together for NNC. For whatever reason they accepted me to the college. So, now I had to save a lot of money in a short amount of time.

I got a job at the gold mine as a geologist's assistant. I made $6.50 an hour. It was a cool job. I got an apartment in town with Jamie and ate nothing but peanut butter and jelly sandwiches for months so I could save money. Phyllis would invite me over for Sunday lunch. She acted like it was no big deal to give me food, but it was the only real nutrition I got. I was so thankful. I always made sure to wash the dishes and help clean up afterwards. After a while I moved out and needed a place to stay for a month. Phyllis insisted that I stay with her in the extra bedroom until I got another place. There was always somebody staying at her house. She wouldn't let me pay her any rent either.

I learned so much at the gold mine. I didn't work in the mine itself. I worked in exploration. It was our job to find the gold that they would one day dig up. It is a tedious process. We had to survey this entire mountain and put stakes in every 100 feet in a giant grid. We had to label everything and keep track of it and make charts and topographical maps. Then we had to take soil samples at every stake. We had to dig into old dirt and take out a small sack of it from every stake and label those as well. Then they would send the soil samples off to the assayer who would tell us what elements were in each sample.

Then we had to drill hundreds of feet into the earth with core drills and take core samples. We had holes everywhere at every possible angle. They had all the holes mapped out as well. Then we had to split the core samples in half by hand. One half would go to the assayer and the other half would go to the geologists who would then determine where the gold might be. We kept all the core samples in archives, which were huge. The cost was monumental!

One day all the geologists got very excited because they had found "visible gold" in one of the core samples. They showed us. We were naive and pointed and said we saw it. They laughed and said, "No, that's pyrite, fool's gold" The real gold is right here. They got out a needle and a magnifying glass and pointed at this microscopic dull flake. I said "That's it?" and then I learned a valuable lesson, one that has stuck with me through the years.

The days of getting gold nuggets off the ground or in a stream are long gone. A gold mine takes a lot of work to set up, as you can tell. Once we find where the gold might be we have to blast the rock out and go miles below the surface of the earth. Then we bring the blasted rock to the surface and pulverize it. The good stuff we put in huge vats and extracted all the metals. We skim all the metals off and put those in another vat where we refine it again and again and again until we are left with pure gold. In a good gold mine we would only get a tenth of an ounce of gold out of every ton of rock! With three shifts working around the clock we only get two 80-pound gold bricks a week if we were doing well. It cost $80 million just to set up the gold mine we were working on.

It hardly seemed worth it to me. It seemed so hopeless. All that work and all that money for a tenth of an ounce of gold! Later I did the math. It was about $2 million a week. All of the sudden it made sense to me. And then I saw it. We are like that! God says we are like gold refined in the fire seven times. It takes great expense and work just to map out where the gold might be in us. Then we have to be tested just to see if there is a sample of what God is looking for, if there is even hope for us.

Then we have to dig deep within us far below the surface, miles below the surface. Farther than any person would ever want to go. Then we have to be blasted out of our comfort zone. And then we have to be pulverized. We have to be broken down to nothing so that the treasure can be found. Then we have to be tried by fire, which for us the fire is usually unpleasant circumstances and trials.

This has to happen again and again and again until we are left with only pure gold. Without all that we are only a pile of rocks. He only puts the good stuff in the fire to be purified though. The trash rock is just discarded immediately. No real trial, it just sits there. I looked back and realized that is what God has been doing with me! All my trials and temptations, all the trials by fire are only purifying me. So break me God, test me, try me until I am what you want me to be. I am yours! I will come out of this whole thing shining, watch and see!

All that work and expense and time and hassle is worth it in the end. One day the trials that were so hard for me when I was going through them will be jewels in my crown. The real challenge is to know that *while* we are actually going through the trial. In retrospect, we can always see how even the bad things in life had a purpose. How they worked out for good in the long run. So if we know that, then we can apply it while we are going through the hard times. We can hold our head up high and say this is all for a good reason and I won't complain. It is hard at first, but very effective... if you can do it.

One of Phyllis' favorite scriptures is Romans 8:28 which says, *"For we know that ALL things work together for the good of those who love him and are called according to his purpose."* That's right. ALL things. Even the bad ones are there for your good! What a blessing!

After a few months the work ran out for me at the gold mine. We had found the gold. They ended up starting a new gold mine there. To my knowledge they are still digging on it to this day. But my job was done. Republic had two gold mines and a sawmill. I like variety so I applied to the sawmill. I got the job. That place was huge!

I remember the first day on the job. I had to be there at 4 in the morning. I was wearing all this gear that was awkward for me. I had a hardhat, chaps, steel-toed boots with heels, gloves, long sleeve shirt and pants, and earplugs. I had to park about a quarter of a mile from where I actually had to work. So, I parked and then I walked and walked and walked in this silly looking outfit. I walked past huge, loud machinery that I didn't understand past rough looking, hard-working, jaded people. I realized how small I was. The whole thing intimidated me. Inside I wanted to go back home and just not try, but I walked on. I found my way and I started working. It was amazing to me that someone had invented all this machinery.

I started on the green chain. Basically, I sorted all the extra boards straight out of the sawmill that the automatic sorter didn't get to. There were 30 bins to sort into and a huge set of chains pulled the lumber across all the bins. I would walk up and down a catwalk and sort the boards as they got to the right bin. The lumber was still "green" because it hadn't been kiln-dried yet. So, it was called the "green chain". The sawmill was very interesting to me. When I wasn't doing my job I would go to different stations and see how their equipment worked. I wanted to learn all about this stuff. It was so cool.

The whole thing was so huge and complicated and yet when you looked closely at any one part it was really very simple. That is the way it is with anything though. Complicated things are just a bunch of simple things put together. You just have to look long enough to understand the pattern and get the big picture. There were laser guided saws and computerized sorting machines. There were conveyer belts and chains and vibrating bins. There were debarking machines and chippers. The whole thing had an organized chaos to it. I really learned a lot.

After a few days I wasn't intimidated any more. I was a part of it. I think it was a big step for me in my confidence. You see a man has to feel like he is a man. He has to have some sense of victory. It is a right of passage. He has to measure up. If he doesn't then he is just a coward until he does. Most men never really get the opportunity to do anything truly challenging and so they never feel whole inside. They spend the rest of their lives trying to measure up, but always feeling like if anyone saw the real them that they would be exposed for the phonies they really were. So they hide. They put other people down to try to make themselves feel better. I am blessed. I have been challenged in life time and time again. I have been broken and rebuilt more times than I can count.

Anyway, I made $7 an hour at the sawmill. I worked there for a few months and saved some more money for college. I learned a lot and gained some self-respect, which I needed. I finally felt like I had something to offer the world besides just labor and food service. In the fall of 1991 I packed my things and went to college in Nampa, Idaho at Northwest Nazarene College. There were three of us from Republic. I felt so inferior it was unbelievable. I hadn't been in school for three years and I was a dropout. Mike was going to take Calculus and Chemistry and Physics and a bunch of other smart classes. He was going to be on the basketball team and do lots of extra-curricular activities. I was going to TRY to pass. I wanted to be a pastor so I could preach the gospel to people who needed it. I was going to work hard so that I could hopefully make enough money to cover my second and third terms. I just hoped I could keep up and maybe even possibly pass.

6 College Makes You Smart?

I thought the sawmill had intimidated me, but that was just labor work. Now I was in college! I couldn't help feeling like a fish out of water. After all I was a loser dropout who was clearly not college material, but I wanted to preach the gospel. I wanted to share my faith with people who needed help. And so, if this was what I had to do to be able to do that then I would do it with all my heart. And if I failed... then at least I tried. I moved into my dorm room. A lot of the people there had been preparing their whole lives for college. They knew who their roommates would be. They had matching furniture and sheets. They had college funds. Not me. Thank God. I appreciated the opportunity and felt blessed to get to be there at all, despite my past. When I went to college, my mother bought me some laundry detergent and deodorant and she said, "I know you are going to do well. I believe in you." That is worth more than any college fund to me.

I met my roommate. He was a lot of fun. His name was Kyle. We got along great. We didn't sleep much. We stayed up way too late every night talking about life and what we would be and what our goals were and girls and whatever else came to mind. We were also prank kings in the school. The great thing about being poor is that you have to be creative, which seems to be harder for rich people. You have to learn how to make it on nothing somehow, so you do. It is fun.

I was there to learn to preach, but I only got to take a few religion classes. I had to take a bunch of required classes. If I had it to do over I would have just taken what interested me instead. I wasted so much time learning pointless stuff that I will never use. I did learn a lot, however. The most important lesson I learned is that college people weren't any smarter than me. They were just in school a little longer because they had the opportunity to be there. Most of them barely scraped by and only went because their parents made them. However, they will get the "good jobs" because of that precious piece of paper. Of course there are some people who actually apply themselves and have some natural talent, but overall I was unimpressed with the intelligence of the "educated idiots".

I also learned that it was harder for me to try to live a Christian life when surrounded by Christians at a Christian school. Out in the real world if someone is messed up they usually know it and deep down they are searching for an answer to their problems. They may not say it, but inside they know they are lost. I can live with that. Honest people. They may laugh at me or tell me to shut up... or they may listen. Either way, they aren't pretending. In a church or Christian school it isn't that cut and dry. Everyone knows the right things to say and do in the presence of the right people, but their actions a lot of the time are much worse then the "worldly people" and the "heathens". They tend to be hypocrites, but they don't even see it. You can't really tell someone he is a hypocrite. And how do they know to change if they don't think there is a problem?

The same thing happened with the early church. Christians were persecuted and killed for their faith from the time of Jesus until 330 A.D. Naturally, if you are willing to die for saying something you think long and hard before you profess it publicly. There had to be a real change in someone for them to say they were a Christian at all. This weeded out a lot of the hypocrites and people teetering on the edge. Christians were fed to the lions and wild animals, they were burned alive, they were crucified, they were beaten, cut in two, and so on. Their testimony to the world was that they wouldn't renounce their faith even in the face of death.

As the lions would be running at them they would calmly stand and sing praises to God. Without fear they would stand in the face of danger. And the world stood by and watched as they were murdered. But the world stood in awe! What kind of a man gives no thought for his life when it can be bought just by denying their God? What kind of person would rather die than betray Jesus? A Christian! That's who. Someone who has been bought with the blood of Jesus and knows they are no better then their master. Someone who knows that their killers don't hate him, but Jesus in him. That is powerful! And so instead of shrinking, their numbers grew!

In 330 A.D. Constantine declared the entire Roman Empire to be Christian. The Romans were used to having their religion change regularly. If Caesar said worship me, the people would... or they would die. If he said to worship a Greek or Roman god or goddess they would, or they would die. If he said to worship an iron statue they would and if he said to worship Jesus they did that too. The Roman Empire dissolved and the Roman Catholic Church was born. All of the sudden everyone professed to be a Christian and said all the right things, but their hearts were far from God. Christianity sadly became what it never should have been... a religion.

I do not doubt that people mean well. Just like they meant well with the Crusades and so many other crimes against humanity done in the name of God. My point is that when everyone thinks *they* are the chosen people and that everyone else is going to hell, bad things happen. I would rather be in a place where we are ***all*** struggling to find the right path and we can admit that we could be wrong. I would rather be in a place where the way you treat people is more important than what doctrine you adhere to. Few people really know the doctrine of the church they go to and it is a rare thing to find someone who actually lives what they believe. That is the true test of faith, though! You should never have to say a word. You should write your faith, with no words, upon your sleeve, and by your actions everyone will know what you believe. Speak only if you are asked.

Enough about that, I had to take this filler class to be considered a fulltime student in the third term. It was called "Camp Counseling Outdoor Education". I remember almost nothing about that class except this. The professor said, **"You have a responsibility to everyone around you. There is always someone looking up to you. There is always someone who idolizes you and watches your every move. There is always someone falling in love with your smile. No matter who you are or how insignificant you may feel. There is always someone who sees you as their hero, and it usually is NOT the person you think."**

Wow! How profound, but how simple and true! I know that there were people that I looked up to that probably didn't know that I watched them, so there must be people that do the same thing to me without my knowledge. People that seem tough on the outside, but are searching desperately for answers inside. Fragile people who don't want you to know that they are watching you because they want to see you for who you really are. I have noticed that people always talk when the Christian falls. On the outside you hear them say condescending things about how we are all hypocrites and that nobody really does what they believe anyway so why even bother trying. Don't trust anyone because they are all dirty...just like us.

It seems that everyone is watching for the Christian to fall, but I think deeper down it is because they all want the Christian to succeed. They want to see someone really believe and act on it. They want to know it can be done... so they can try as well. Since we are all sheep no one wants to be the first. So we all stutter around aimlessly desperately hoping inside that someone will show us the way to live and show us the way home. That statement was worth the whole year. I will never forget that.

To this day I live my life as if I am constantly being watched...especially when I'm alone. I try to live with integrity so as to set an example. This doesn't mean I always do, but I am quick to admit my shortcomings and as soon as I find them out I make every effort to try to overcome them. You see when you fall; you never fall alone. And when you stand you don't just stand for yourself. We all impact each other, for better or for worse. If I leave a mark on this world, which we all do, I want it to be a positive one.

I had a Biblical Literature professor who challenged me a lot. He started off by saying that he was the hardest Bib/Lit professor there. We all sighed a little inside. Then he said "I will challenge you and you will work hard, but I will remember every one of your names and you will remember mine, and the stuff you learn in my class will stay with you for the rest of your life." He was a man of his word. He remembered all of our names. He videotaped us all saying our names the first day of class and watched it at home. He really seemed to care. To this day I still remember his name. And, just like he said, the stuff I learned in that class has stuck with me for the rest of my life. We had to read the entire Bible for that class. Normally, I had no problem doing less then what I was told as long as I still passed, but not in this class. I was there to learn the Bible, so I did everything he said. I read the whole Bible again, I wrote long papers, I studied, and I memorized all the books of the Bible and their content and their history. I learned "why" to a lot of questions that most people have. I am so grateful that he pushed us. Thank you, George.

As you can probably tell college wasn't quite as difficult as I thought it would be. In fact I thought it was pretty easy really. At the beginning of each term they gave you a syllabus that told you exactly what you would have to do all term. You knew from day one when you had papers to write or projects to finish. It made it pretty easy for me. Once I got in the groove for each class and felt out what kind of professor I had to please, I would just start chipping away little by little at the projects and papers. I would be done weeks before they were ever expected. Everyone else would wait until the last minute and then act surprised like the professor just made it up to throw them off.

I learned to use small blocks of time wisely. In one of my classes they told us to write down everything we did in a week. Everyone said they had no time to study. We all had to sleep, we all had classes and some of us had jobs, extra curricular activities, and recreation which seemingly added up to no time at all to study. But even with a full schedule we all had lots of free hours of doing absolutely nothing. In between classes we would just waste time. People acted like they needed to have 6 hours to study all in a row. They told us that if you study in smaller blocks of time that you retain more of the information, you aren't as fatigued, and you get done a lot more than you ever thought you could. So, I applied that theory to my life. They were right! If I had 30 minutes in between classes I would do part of an assignment or read a chapter or something. I found that I always had lots of free time. I seemed to study a lot less than everyone else. And I got the highest GPA in my class and department. I got a 3.97! Not bad for a loser dropout, huh?

Since I still didn't have a driver's license or a car I had to work on campus...doing food service. I made $4.25 an hour, half what I made at the sawmill. I didn't let that stop me. I was a machine at work! I picked up every shift I could. I got an award for "Sub of the Year" at my job. I washed dishes, cooked, cleaned, did banquets, folded napkins, served thankless people, took out the trash, mopped, and so on. I learned a lot. The Bible says the greatest among you shall be the servant of all. This can be taken three ways; 1) you could say ha, my boss will be the servant one day or 2) you could say that the guy doing the menial tasks is the greatest among us or 3) you could say that the guy who is the greatest among us already knows his place so he has nothing to prove to anyone. He is ok doing little things because he already knows he is something great.

I think that is what Jesus meant. You see he is God. He is the greatest among us, but he washed the disciples feet. This was considered the lowest person's job. Either way, it was a little humbling. I was happy to do it. I did my job as unto the Lord. I learned a lot. I made enough money to get me most of the way through the year. The last term I had to borrow $1,000 from my grandfather who later told me not to bother paying him back. I was very grateful for that.

Then there were all the fun parts of college! Because I studied in between classes and work, I always had a lot of free time when it came time to have fun. Plus, I didn't have to feel guilty that I was falling behind. One of the things we would do all the time is go out to a place called Jump Creek. It was a drive, but it was so fun! There was this creek that ran through a canyon. There were cliffs and waterfalls and valleys and caves. It was great! We would go rock climbing. We swam in the pool at the bottom of the waterfall. We would explore all over the place. While we were out there we could forget about school and life for a little while and just let loose. We risked our lives several times. In case you are wondering, you never really live until you risk your life... at least a little. Personally, I like to push the limits!

We would talk while we were on the trails about all kinds of deep things. There is nothing more breathtaking for me than being in high places. I love it! When it got dark, we would build a fire and roast hotdogs and marshmallows. We would bring out the acoustic guitars and sing and play and laugh. I loved that place. Some people would drink. I wouldn't. We went every chance we got. I wish I had gone more.

One day some military group had repelling off of our 7-story science building for free! We were all there. What a rush! You have to back up off a building while you are seventy feet off the ground and trust the rope and the guy holding it. I went as many times as I could. I love heights!

We also used to go "ice-blocking". This guy had a huge house at the top of this giant grassy hill. We would go to the grocery store and buy a block of ice for a dollar. We would climb to the top of the hill, put a folded towel on the ice block, sit on it, cross our feet, lean back, and fly down this grassy hill. It was so fun! You would wreck sometimes, but it didn't hurt that bad. Once you got to the bottom, you had to hike all the way back up. We did that a lot too. It's amazing how much fun you can have for a dollar.

I had kept my hair short because I was trying to be a pastor. One day there was a concert. I got to feed the bands because I worked at the food court. I found out about the show and got there early to help load equipment. I got right up front when the concert started. Half way through the show the band said, " Now it is time for audience participation." They picked some girl out of the audience and then they picked me! We got up on stage and the lead singer looks at me and says, "Well, do something." So I said "Do what?" He said "Anything." so I was like "Anything?" and he said "Yeah, anything." So I looked at him and said, "Let me see his guitar." They were so stunned that they gave me the guitar.

I played around for a second and then started playing a song I had written called "Alone in the Dark". The crowd started going crazy. I knew a lot of the people there. I was in a band and everyone knew that. So then the bass player and drummer of this famous band started playing along with ME. I was singing and playing and they were playing with me. The crowd was going nuts. I got to the third chorus and the singer put his hand on my back. He said, "Dude, my manager is mad at me because you are getting more attention then we are. Can you stop?" So, I did. It was so cool though. There were thousands of people there. It was great! That night I realized that if I wanted to play in a band I would have to look a certain way to appeal to the people. They don't just want anybody from the crowd on the stage. They want something different, something amazing. So, I started growing my hair out again that night.

Remember my friend Mike that was so confidant when we went to college; the one that took Calculus and Physics, and all that. He dropped out after one term with a 0.17 GPA. Amazing isn't it? Lots of people dropped out. The class got smaller and smaller as the year went on. Then my turn came.

As the year came to a close I did the math for the next year's finances. There was no way I could afford it **unless** I lived off campus and ate my own food. Room and board was expensive there! I looked through the rulebook for the school. I found out that if you had been out of high school for three years or more then you could live off campus. So, I went to my counselor and told him my concern. I told him that I wanted to preach with all my heart, but I couldn't afford school unless they would let me live off campus. I would gladly sacrifice and eat Ramon noodles everyday if they would just let me. He refused.

So, I appealed. Everyone turned me down. I appealed right up to the president of the college. I finally told them "I have the highest GPA in my class and department. I am a good student. In fact, according to your numbers, I am the best. I have lived on my own for the last three years. Please, let me live off campus so I can still come here." The guy looked at me smugly and said, "That rule wasn't made for dropouts like you." I told him they would lose me as a student if I had to live on campus. He shrugged carelessly and thanked me for my time. I was devastated!

Jesus said of the Pharisees that they strain at a gnat, yet they swallow the camel. In other words they are concerned with all the petty unimportant things, but they miss the point. They missed the point that day. What a terrible thing it is to break the will of an eager heart. I could have used that as an excuse to fall, but a long time before that I had resolved to never let someone else's hypocrisy make me into a hypocrite. So, I decided to do home study. It was a lot cheaper and I could go at my own pace, which is fast!

I left NNC a better man than I came. I learned a lot. Not just book knowledge. I learned a lot about me! I learned that I could do *anything* I set my mind to. It was like I had been validated. A man needs to have some sense of dignity and self-respect. I had always thought of myself as a loser and a dropout. To this day I joke about being a loser and a dropout, but it is only a joke. I know that I am a success, and so does everyone around me. I don't have to brag because it is painfully obvious to everyone I meet. It was worth the $10,000 I paid to have that. I had a blast! I got to be a kid again. It was a lot of fun.

I drove back to Republic, Washington with my head held a little higher. I got a job at the sawmill again. I moved in with a friend of mine named Jeff. He went to my church and he played guitar and we worked at the sawmill together. We had a lot of fun.

7 Now What?

When I started working for the sawmill again they put me on the planer side of the mill, instead of the sawmill side. I caught on quickly and had some experience already. They decided that I had potential so they decided to make me a floater. They trained me how to do every job in the planer so that I could cover for anyone that was sick. They also trained me how to drive a forklift. I was given the worst forklift in the world to learn on and the conditions weren't much better. For those of you who don't know, a forklift has three pedals: gas, a brake, and a clutch/brake. The clutch brake disengages the wheels from the gas so that you can give it gas while you are lifting something heavy without moving forward, even though you are in gear. It is something you use all day long as a forklift driver. This one particular clutch/brake wasn't really functional. Every time you would release it the whole machine would jerk back and forth violently. My job was to pick up unbanded, poorly stacked units of lumber and carry them across thirty sets of tracks (like railroad tracks, very bumpy) over to the stacker machine, which would then stack it neatly. Between the clutch/brake, the thirty sets of bumpy tracks, and the poorly stacked lumber I was dropping loads all the time. Not to mention that the guy teaching me was not a good teacher at all. His name was Hec, short for Hector. He had been kicked in the head more than once by horses and bulls in the rodeo. He dipped snuff and was very cocky. He had that "My brain's not here right now" look on his face all the time.

My first day of training was humiliating. I was ready to give up. I thought they had made a big mistake by picking me to do this job. All night I dreamed of frustrating scenarios with my forklift. I was trying to move loads of lumber through my bedroom, but they wouldn't fit through the door. I had to keep moving them around to try to make room. The whole thing seemed impossible. It was. I was dreaming. Finally, I woke up and thought about the situation. Then it hit me. Hec is an idiot and he can drive a forklift! If he can do it, I can! I went in the next day and I learned to drive that forklift well. I didn't get frustrated or give up, no matter what. Ever since then I have always used that analogy. Anything I feel is impossible, I simply look at the people who are doing it already and I say to myself "Hec can do it and he is an idiot. If he can do it I can!" And then I do it. Every time.

In fact the Bible says that all the prophets and the great men that we esteem were men just like us, common men. We aren't born heroes. Men like you and me have made this world what it is because we believe it can be done and we don't give up until it is done. We have put people on the moon because someone believed it could be done, and they didn't give up until they were there. That is a perfect example of faith in action. In James it says that faith without works is dead. Just like the body is without the soul, so is faith dead without works. What if they just believed it could be done, but never tried? We wouldn't be there, would we? And I want to be there. So, I will not give up until I succeed... or die trying.

I became one of the best forklift drivers the sawmill had. I learned all the jobs there. I was always fascinated with the inner workings of the whole thing, so it was fun for me to learn more and more. If you do your job with your whole heart the day goes by quicker and you are happier, plus you get noticed and you get raises. It is a win-win situation.

There was a guy that had been working the same station for 15 years! It was so boring! All he did was watch boards go by and make sure there wasn't a "wreck". About twice a day there was a wreck so he hit an emergency stop button and fixed the problem and then started everything up again. He sat there drinking coffee and smoking cigarettes and looking depressed and jittery all the time. You couldn't really talk that much because it was so loud in there. It was like he didn't even have a personality any more. It was very sad. I think there are a lot of people like that in the world. Don't they want to do more? I do. It is your choice you know. No one is going to force you to do something cool with your life.

Lots of the guys at the sawmill were missing fingers or had bad scars from industrial accidents. Some of them were "accidents" and some of them were "on purposes". Sometimes we would have spikes that the tree-huggers would nail in the trees mess up our saws. The saw blades, which were enormous, would shred and fly everywhere. It was very dangerous. People got hurt. Sometimes stuff just happens if people are careless. Some of the guys would cut off fingers or get hurt on purpose though. Insurance has a dollar amount for each injury. If you lose your pinkie finger up to the first knuckle you get a certain amount, but if it goes to the second knuckle you get more. So, if a guy was desperate he would cut off a little of his left pinkie finger and get about $70,000 or so. The money will spend and be gone quickly, but the finger will never grow back! Apparently they would encourage each other to be brave when the time came. That was disturbing to me. If you get hurt by accident that is one thing, but why would you do it on purpose?

Once you had an accident they couldn't fire you because you could say that it was discrimination for the handicap. So, the guys that had missing parts didn't do anything at all. One of them slept on the job everyday and nobody would say anything to him because his arm had gotten caught in some machinery and gotten torn up pretty bad. I don't think he did it on purpose, but why not just do your job so everyone else doesn't have to pick up your slack?

When I wasn't working I would study. I read all the books I was supposed to for home study to be a pastor. I took all the tests. I worked hard. I also was very involved in church. I got to be a Sunday school teacher for every different age group from infant to adult at some point or another. I got to preach, and sing, and usher, and teach in the church. I learned a lot. I also learned about church politics, which interest me about as much as eating broken glass. I know they have their place, I guess, but I don't have to like it. Come to think of it I don't actually know anyone who likes church politics, not even the ones who enforce them. Weird isn't it?

One of the cool things I did was take a class in church on financial planning. I couldn't have cared less about financial planning at the time, but I pretty much went to every church function at the time. I am so glad I took that class. I learned so much. There were a few highlights. 1) Never buy anything you can't pay cash for 2) If possible, wait at least 30 days before making a major purchase to avoid impulse buys and unnecessary items 3) Set a financial ceiling for yourself. This was the most interesting thing for me. You see no matter how much money people make they always seem to be struggling. It is because they always spend more than they make. If you can survive on $20,000 a year then you can survive on $50,000 a year, right? But the people making $50,000 a year are struggling as much as the guy making $20,000 a year. Why? Because we are never satisfied with what we have, that's why. We always spend more than we have. It is our nature.

Set a standard of living that you are comfortable with. Anything you make above that save it, invest it, or give it away and you will always be rich, content, and happy. I applied that to my life and it is so true. It has helped me so much with money management. Someone said to me, "but you only make $20,000 a year. How are you supposed to live on that?" I thought "if someone handed me $20,000 for my year all at one time would I spend it on the stupid things I spend it on now? Probably not. So, how is it any different if it trickles in across a year? It isn't. It is the same amount of money either way." I chose to use my money wisely. So I lived like I didn't have any at all. I was a lot happier and more content then the people around me. When I did want something I had already saved for it so I just got it and didn't have to worry.

It really is a great way to live. I highly recommend it. If you really do have money than you shouldn't care what people think of you. It is only the wannabe that has something to prove. The people showing the most flash are the ones struggling the most. Ironic isn't it? In fact the average millionaire lives well below their means. If you didn't know they were rich you would never guess it. It makes sense, ask around. You'll be surprised. Here's more interesting trivia: Did you know that 40% of homeowners own their home outright? In other words they have completely paid for their homes. They don't owe anything to the bank or anyone else for that matter. I didn't think that was true until I asked around and it is true.

Back to the story, River had been living in North Carolina this whole time by himself. He came up to visit my mom, who had moved to another town in Washington so I went to visit her as well. My hair had grown a little. His hair had grown a lot! It was down to his waist. He had learned a lot about music theory. He knew his scales and modes. He was amazing! He had his bass with him and played some stuff. I was impressed. Of course I had been playing guitar and writing songs as well. He had decided to clean up his life and get off drugs. He was in a Christian band.

We discussed the possibility of merging our talents into one band. It seemed like I could reach a lot of people through music. It had always been a strength of mine. I always related well to the underdog or the losers or druggies partly because I had been there and I want to help and partly because fake people drive me insane. The lower class is down to earth. What you see is what you get. It may not be pretty, but it is real. Poor people are transparent. I like that.

Every winter the sawmill would lay a bunch of people off because of the snow. They would go on unemployment until work picked up again and then they would come back. It started getting slow and so I took a voluntary layoff. I figured I would get some unemployment money to get me through for a while and move down to North Carolina with River and join his band. I had saved a lot of money. I guess a lot is relative, isn't it? For a long time I had been riding a bike to work. I finally got my driver's license when I was 18 years old. Later I bought a 1988 Hyundai Excel for about $2,000. I paid cash for it, of course. I was making $9.79 an hour at the time, which was more than I had ever made. Plus I had saved about $1,000 on top of that. I would laugh at that now, but it was a big deal at the time.

So, I packed everything I owned into my little car and I drove to North Carolina. I stopped on the way and visited my mom and then I went to NNC to say hi to everyone. The rest of the drive was insane! It took four days total, including the two stops to visit people. The last day I drove 21 hours straight! I was so tired and strung out. I was slaphappy and silly and sore. I showed up at River's apartment at 3am. I saw a lot of cool things on the way like road signs and lines on the road (some of them had dotted lines), there were also a lot of cars on the road.

River and I caught up on old times and the next day I went and got a job as a painter. I had to lower my rate of pay to $7 an hour. After a week or so I realized that everyone I worked with wanted to get high and huff paint all the time, so I quit that job. Then I got a job putting on high-rise roofs. That was fun! I learned a lot, and like I said I like heights a lot. It can be a little scary and dangerous at times, but the rush is the fun of it.

On my first day on the job I climbed up a three-story scaffold. It really wasn't that high and I wasn't afraid, but as I looked at the roof it started spinning around in circles. It wasn't like I was sick; it was like the roof really was spinning. I stopped myself. I knew that couldn't be true, so I looked again. It wasn't the roof or me; it was the scaffolding that was spinning. It wasn't really spinning either it was just kind of rocking back and forth in a circular pattern. All that happened in a split second, by the way. It is weird how your mind can play tricks on you like that. They say that deja vu happens when your present experience goes straight to your memory banks and bypasses whatever else it needs to hit first. So then it seems like we remember it happening just like this before, but it is only happening once.

I learned how to work safely in high places. I learned how to work with metal and roofing material. I learned how to think like water so that we could keep the leaks out. I overcame any fear of heights I might have had left. And I got a lot of cool stories. I also saw a lot of people get hurt. The owner of the company fell 50 feet through a skylight. He hit every beam and piece of steel he could on the way down. He died. Another guy let his seventeen-year-old son up on a roof. He fell through a skylight 50 feet also. He landed on his feet, but he broke both his legs and his knees broke both sides of his jaw. Not fun.

Another guy fell 50 feet and used his hammer to claw enough friction in the wall on the way down that he only got a little banged up. I was on an eight story parking garage one day. They took me off that job to work on a middle school the next day. The guy that replaced me the next day fell off that 8 story parking garage and died. We heard it on the radio. Roofing can be dangerous. Fortunately, I never got hurt. In Psalms 37: 23-24 it says "If the Lord delights in a man's way he makes his steps firm; though he stumble, ***he will not fall***, for the Lord upholds him with his hand."

I have always claimed that scripture as a roofer. I have stumbled many times. I have had many close calls. I have even fallen off of several roofs. But I have never been hurt badly. I live without fear because I know whose hands I am in. I have found that no matter how hard you try if it isn't your time to go, then it isn't your time to go. I know a guy that put a double barrel shotgun in his mouth and pulled the trigger. He blew half his face off, but didn't die. So, he pulled the trigger again for the second shot. It misfired, again and again and again. He couldn't get the gun to work for the death of him. It wasn't his time. Later he shot a man five times in the chest and went to jail. In jail he found the Lord and was born again. God had another plan for Dave's life.

On the contrary, no matter how hard you try if it is your time there is nothing you can do to escape the hand of God. Try all you like. When your number is up, that's it. That might be discouraging for some, but not for me. You see for me to live is Christ and to die is gain. I want to go home more than anything in the world. I would give everything I have to be home. I am like a fish out of water here, gasping on the beach because I am not made for this. When I do go home I will sing for joy, loud and long. You will hear it down here. The corners of my mouth will touch in the back of my head because I will be smiling so big!

So, I am not afraid to die. I can dance on the edge of life and death and danger, all the while knowing that either way I am OK. A long time ago I asked God to take me home as soon as I became useless to Him here. So, every morning I wake up I realize that there must be more for me to do. I must have more usefulness left in me. God must need me for something today, so I look for that something. I look for a way to be used that would put a smile on His face and that would bless people. At any time I am totally content with dropping everything and going home to heaven, but until that moment I refuse to live in fear of anyone or anything.

I am free, but I am bought with a price. I will not waste the talent I have been given. I will not cower away from my duty. There are no cowards in heaven. In Revelation 21:7-8 it says: " He who overcomes will inherit all this, and I will be his God and he will be my son. But the _**cowardly**_, the unbelieving, the vile, the murderers, the sexually immoral, those who practice magic arts, the idolaters and all liars- their place will be in the fiery lake of burning sulfur."

Meanwhile, back at home, our roommate Brian wasn't all we wanted in a roommate or a band mate. One day I needed shampoo and we were out in our bathroom so I went to see if he had any I could use. As I walked through his room I saw the biggest porn collection I think I have ever seen. There were videos everywhere and a crate overflowing with magazines. It was disturbing to say the least. It was all he could talk about. Everything that came out of that guy's mouth was sexual and pornographic and disturbing. He eventually locked himself in his room for a month and would only come out to eat while we were gone.

We had a Bible study in our apartment. One day we all showed up for the Bible study and Brian had plastered porn up on the walls in the living room. He degenerated quickly and we saw it. He wouldn't talk to us or answer the door when we knocked. It was weird to say the least. We got the feeling he was about to leave us with all the bills and just disappear. River and I talked about it. We didn't like being there anyway. We decided that we were young and free. We could go anywhere and do anything we wanted. We could move down the road or to the other end of the world. Anything was possible for us.

We had lived in Arlington before and our friend James had moved to Dallas. We heard there was a "heavenly metal" scene there. So we quit our jobs, packed all our stuff into my little car, and drove to Texas. I drove the whole trip because River didn't have a license yet. It was raining hard and I drove without stopping, except for gas.

On the way into Dallas traffic was at a standstill. I didn't see it in time. I hit the brakes, we screeched and squealed to a stop, but not before rear-ending a little old lady in front of us! She got out of her car holding her neck and I knew it was over for me. I had just been in two other wrecks within the last month. (I had pulled out on a blind corner in North Carolina and did $2,700 worth of body damage to some lady's car and I ran over a huge rock in the middle of the road and punctured my gas tank.) The old lady and I talked and, for whatever reason, she let me go. She said there was no damage to her car and she would probably be all right. I could hardly believe it. My car on the other hand had some pretty bad frame damage. I had to turn the wheel all the way to the right just so it would go straight. It cost about $500 of the $700 I had saved to fix it.

We got to James' house and he let us stay with him for two days while we found an apartment and some jobs. He told us to follow him into Arlington, so I did. He drove way too fast and at the last minute cut out of a lane in traffic. I couldn't get out in time because there was a car next to me. I hit the curb and popped my tire and bent my rim. James didn't stop because he hadn't seen it so I had to chase him down with my broken tire. This was way before cell phones. When he finally did stop I got out to fix the tire, but my spare was under everything we owned. I was a little frustrated that night. I threw the tire down on the ground and it bounced out into the highway. Thankfully, we caught the tire before any damage was done. I finally got it all fixed and luckily nobody was hurt.

We got a one-bedroom apartment that was two apartment complexes away from the one my old dealer lived in (the one who got busted right in front of me). River did food service, as usual. I saw an ad to "Be a manager for $40,000 a year, long hairs OK." I had long hair and I wouldn't mind making $40,000 a year so I went and applied. It was a scam. I solicited copycat perfume to people who didn't want it. I think I made about $27 in a week, and then I quit.

I found a job as a roofer putting on aluminum roofs. They are expensive so we only worked for rich people. Rich people are very picky. I got used to doing work for picky people. I often wanted to tell them how lucky they were to have any of this stuff at all. I wanted to invite them to our one bedroom apartment where we both slept on the floor with no air conditioning, but I held my tongue. I did what I was told and once again I learned a lot.

On December 7th, 1992 we went to East Park Church of the Nazarene for the first time. I saw a girl across the church that was beautiful. She was outgoing and fun and she was a leader in the church. Her name was Lana. She introduced herself to me and stuck out her hand. I was very impressed. After church everyone was milling around. I wanted to talk to her, but this guy wouldn't leave me alone. Finally I turned around right in front of a group of strangers and said, "Do you want to go out tomorrow night?" She was busy. I said what about Friday? Also busy. What about Saturday? Saturday was good. Maybe I was brave? Or maybe I had been single for four years and didn't want to pass up an opportunity to see this gorgeous girl again.

Back when River and I had been doing drugs we had some friends named Bobby and Justin and Bruce. Bruce was my age (19) and the other two were River's age (17). When I had gotten saved 3 years earlier I had talked to them about Jesus. When we came back to Texas they had become Christians as well. We had Bible studies and hung out a lot. We all encouraged each other. River joined their band. I was busy. Anyway, Saturday finally came and it turns out Lana lived almost across the street from Bruce and Justin. It was weird. We talked all day and seemed to have everything in common. We got along great. I was very happy. I was in love!

Lana and I saw each other every day from then on. I think I proposed to her within about a week of going out. I just knew she was the one. The problem was that she was seventeen and still in high school and I was nineteen. I didn't see it as a problem. I was willing to wait anyway. By the time I was her age I had lived on my own for years, lived a lot, died once, been to hell, and built my first house, and everything else you have just read. Seventeen was a ripe old age to me. I often forget that other people have normal lives.

Lana's dad didn't like me at all. I think a big part of it was my hair. He thought I was a loser. One day he needed some help on a job (he owned an erosion control company). We dug ditches, and wheel barrowed dirt, and hauled and dumped heavy loads all day. I never slowed down. That night I had dinner at their house. Lana eagerly asked, "So, how did John do today?" Her dad knew he couldn't say anything bad so instead he grumpily said, "Well, everyone has their gifts, and I guess John's is with dirt." That was his idea of a compliment. Oh well. I knew I did a good job, no matter what he said. He seemed to lighten up a little after that. I guess he respected me a little more after he saw my work ethic.

Then her mom decided to hate me. I don't even remember why. She just did. Her parents tried to forbid her to see me. That didn't work so they told her that she needed to finish high school, finish college, work for a few years, and if she still liked me then we could get married. That would be seven years. After a while they pretended to like me, but it was very fake. I think they just tolerated me. That made for a hard relationship. Why can't people just be happy for you?

I worked like a slave at the roofing company. I got moved up to the best roofing crew they had, with Milton Tunnell. We had the same last name, but we weren't related. He also pronounced it wrong. It is actually Tunnell, with two L's. So it sounds like "Ton El", not tunnel like a hollowed out spot in a mountain. He said with his Southern accent "Yeah, Daddy always said it was supposed to pronounced Tunnell, but we always just thought it was easier to say tunnel." Another guy I worked with laughed and said "Why would you pronounce your own name wrong? 'Yeah, daddy always said it was supposed to be Rosenbower, but we just thought it would be easier to say Smith!' " That was an ongoing joke for the rest of the time I worked there.

By the time I was done working there I was making $8.50 an hour. We had been working off of a hailstorm from a few years back and the work finally ran out. By this time I had been made the youth pastor at East Park Church of the Nazarene. I had gotten my Local Pastor's License. I could marry people and bury people and I could preach. I made $85 a week as a youth pastor. It is great money if you don't like to eat...at all! River and I had moved into the parsonage that the church owned. It was condemned.

There were holes in the roof. Some of the windows were broken. The place was FREEZING COLD, except in the summer when it was BURNING HOT! The water was undrinkable. We had to put water in jugs from Lana's house and drink that. It was hard water... or soft, I don't know really which is which. Either way it was slimy and smelled like sulfur. When you took a shower you never felt clean. You would rinse the soap off, but it always felt like it was still there. It was slimy and gross. The second shower just sprayed water out of the wall and it shocked you if you touched the water, so we didn't go in there.

Looking back it was sub-human. I would never ask anyone to live like that, but at the time I was so very grateful for it. I guess I was really pathetic... or maybe I'm just spoiled now?

I tried really hard to do a good job as a youth pastor. I organized stuff all the time. We had concerts in the fellowship hall. They brought lots of people and everyone had fun. We had lock-ins and outings. We went on a mission trip to Mexico. I thought I had it bad until I went to Mexico. Those people know poverty like I never will. While we were there River and Lana went out to do ministry work and help cook while I stayed back and helped build a church for them. We did a lot in a week. I realized how impatient and ignorant I am about other cultures. I tried to learn their words and communicate, but it was just terrible. It was not a skill set I possessed.

One night, back in Arlington, we had a concert at the church. It was a lot to organize. One of the band members was cold, so I lent him my jacket. He accidentally took it home with him. It changed hands a few times and then ended up at the guitar player's house. After a while I started to get cold without my jacket. I had gotten laid off from roofing earlier that day. I had prayed that God would provide a job that could make at least the $8.50 an hour that I was making and would work around my youth pastor schedule. Two things that I thought would be impossible. So I tracked the jacket down to Jason and asked if I could come get it. It turns out he lived right around the corner from Lana. I drove right over. I had met his dad, Doug, a few times and we started talking.

Doug was a very smart man. He was a pilot and he had owned several companies. He knew something about everything. I told him I had been laid off and jokingly asked him if he needed a new roof. He said "No, but I do need a tile floor laid. Can you do that?" I told him I was willing to do it, but that I had never done it before so I couldn't make any promise as to the outcome." He didn't bat an eye. "There is a free class at Home Depot on how to lay tile. Take the class. If you think you can do it, then I will pay you $10 an hour. I will buy all the tools and the materials, but I get to keep the tools at the end." So, without a thought, I agreed.

I took the class and it was easy. I stripped his linoleum floor in the kitchen, dining room, and laundry room. Then I laid ceramic tile. The next day I grouted it. Doug and Jason were there most of the time. We had a lot of fun. The floor looked great! I was $385 richer. Doug was happy. It was cool. Doug said to me "Maybe this will turn into a business for you? Who knows? You are pretty good at this." I laughed and told him that after this I was going to get a real job. But, before I was done he said he had a neighbor across the street that designed helicopters for a living that needed his house painted. Would I be willing to do the same deal for him: $10 an hour, plus tools and materials?

I agreed. I needed the money, so I worked. When I finished that job there was another friend that wanted some siding repaired. Pretty easy, so yes, I did it. Then the jobs just kept coming. I never stopped working. Every time someone would ask me if I could do something new I would tell them I could take a look. It always seemed pretty easy even if I had never done it before, so I never said no. The jobs got more and more complex, but I just did them. It was challenging sometimes. It was hard work physically, but brain wise it was a piece of cake for me. Every job I did I would say, "after this I'll get a real job." In case you are wondering, I haven't had a real job since. I have been self-employed since I was 20 years old.

On my second job I needed some help so I paid River to help me. I just charged the same $10 an hour for him, but gave him $8 an hour and kept two for myself. He knew and he was just happy to be making $8 an hour. Eventually word got out to the local musicians that I was easy to work for. I never made any promises. I was honest with them. I would say "I know I have enough work to keep you busy for 3 or 4 weeks, beyond that I don't know." Musicians don't think about the long run, so they agreed. I never ran out of work. I didn't advertise or try to get work. I just did the jobs I had time for and I never said no to anyone. It didn't matter how impossible it was I would find a way to make it work.

I got a large customer base pretty quickly and I had lots of repeat business. I remembered every job by the name of the homeowner and so did my crew. We knew the neighbors of our customers. We knew their kids and where they worked. We knew because I cared more about them than the actual job I was there to do. Don't get me wrong I always did my job well, but I always made time for the customer that I was working for. The way I saw it they were spending a lot of money on me and I wanted to make sure they got what they wanted out of the whole thing.

To me it was just common decency and good business, but to everyone else it was groundbreaking to have a contractor who showed up on time, on the day he said he would be there, with no excuses. I did the job in the time I said I would do it, for the price I said I would do it for. I am a man of my word. If I took a loss then I took a loss, but I wouldn't change a price unless they added something that wasn't in the original agreement. We would take our shoes off if we went in their house. We worked hard and fast. We all spoke English and were relatively intelligent. I led my crew by example. There was nothing I would ask them to do that I wasn't willing to do myself, and they knew it. If there were something that was harder or more dangerous I would do that, so that no one else had to risk their lives. My customers told their friends about me. As a result the business prospered. Doug was right. It did turn into quite a business for me.

I learned all about gross profit as opposed to net profit. I learned how to do my taxes. I kept my own books. I was the salesman. I was the problem solver. I was the CPA. I did it all. There was nothing our crew couldn't do. We could build a house from the ground up. And we were all friends. It was great! I was friends with my customers for the most part and I was friends with my crew.

In the meantime Lana and I got engaged. I got her a ring. At first she didn't wear it because she was afraid of what her parents would say. After a little while she told them it was a promise ring so she could wear it around them. They didn't really have anything good to say about me and it seemed like they were always trying to break us up. I ended up remodeling their entire house. I put in hardwood floors and ceramic tile. I redid their cabinets and sinks and faucets. I painted the whole thing inside and out. I built a huge deck with a pool. I put up a new fence and built an office in the backyard. I put fans in everywhere and wallpaper and chair rails. I put in pavestone and a walkway in the backyard. Anything that needed to be fixed, I fixed it. Still, I got no credit.

After Lana graduated she had planned on going to Oklahoma to go to Southern Nazarene University. I had planned on going with her. One night her mother and I had a talk. She forbid me to go to Oklahoma. I tried to be polite, but it eventually came down to this " I am a grown man and I'll go wherever in the world I choose to go with or without your blessing. I love your daughter and we are going to get married. Live with it." I'm pretty sure she never forgave me for that. Women never forget an alleged wrong that was done to them...ever. Years later it was still being brought up.

It came down to the last day. I had resigned as youth pastor. I had wrapped up all my loose ends with the business. I had given notice and packed my stuff. Then Lana said "I don't want you to come to Oklahoma with me. I want to date around and be young and then later we can get married after I get out of college and work a few years." Well, I knew where that had come from. Her parents. It still stung. So, she went alone to college. A few days later she called me up crying. She missed me and wanted me to be there with her. She couldn't believe she had been so foolish. So, I moved to Oklahoma.

8 Archaic Plea

I moved into a one-bedroom apartment one block away from the school. It was the first time in my life I had ever lived alone. I had saved a lot of money, about $5,000 and I had no bills, so that was cool. I did construction up there as well. I raised my rates a few times from $10 to $12 to $15 an hour. I always thought I would lose business by raising my rates and the exact opposite was always true. Every time I raised my rates I got more respect, they complained less, and I got more work. People are funny.

Lana quickly got busy with school and volleyball, so I had a lot of free time. I met a guitar player named Brian and we hit it off pretty quick. We decided to form a band. My hair had gotten pretty long and I had gotten pretty good at playing and singing. We jammed a few times and then found a bass player named Justin (who I called Justin Time or Justin Case) and a drummer named Shawn. We searched for a good band name. We went through a list of them but finally agreed on "Archaic Plea". It was the name of a song I had written and everyone liked it, so it stuck.

Justin, John, Shawn, Brian

We wrote songs like crazy. I wrote songs like crazy. We practiced all the time. We ended up having a Bible study in my apartment twice a week with anyone who wanted to come. It grew quickly! We had lots of people there every week. I bought a pretty big P.A. It took up my whole living room, literally. It went all the way to the ceiling. It took three or four truckloads to haul it every time we played a show. We got to play some cool shows. We played some talent shows and Battle of the Bands. We played a lot of churches and small places that we had to bring our own P.A. We got to record in a million dollar recording studio, which was fun. Our music was on the radio a little and we got interviewed on the radio and a few papers. In retrospect it wasn't that big of a deal, but at the time we felt like rock stars!

I was up at the school so much that everyone thought I went there. So I could just go wherever I wanted and no one said anything. I knew all the codes for the dorms. Every once in a while someone would ask what room I lived in or what classes I was taking and I would laugh and say "I don't go to school here."

After a while Lana made more excuses to not see me. The guys in the band sat me down one night and told me that she was seeing someone else at the school named Bill. Everyone saw them together all the time holding hands and kissing. I stuck up for her. I didn't believe them. I asked her about it and she got upset. She finally came clean, kind of. She said, "I just want to date around a little, that's all. What is the big deal? Why do you have to be so 'all or nothing?' If I would have told you, you would have freaked out."

She broke up with me. I was crushed. I couldn't believe it. The guy was a nerd too! Complete with glasses and pocket protectors. I was the lead singer and guitar player for the most popular band on campus, and in town. I made good money. I was nice. It didn't make sense. I was pretty depressed for a while. I would walk around alone at night and just cry. I really did love her.

The band hung out a lot. We did lots of fun stuff. We would go camping. I would bring the acoustic guitar and sing and play into the night. All the groupies would sing along with our songs. There is nothing as cool as having people sing along to something you wrote. It always takes me a minute to realize that "oh yeah, they shouldn't know this. I wrote that. I mean I know it, but I wrote it. They actually pay attention? That's cool!"

We went to a party one night. At some point someone offered me some drugs or alcohol. I don't remember which. I thanked them, but said no. They asked why not. So, I told them. After a while the whole room was listening to me. It must be a rare thing for someone to stand up for what they believe in I guess, because it happens everywhere I go. Eventually, they turned the music off and everyone wanted to know how I had overdosed and how I had gotten saved. Just like you are reading right now. I still just shrug and say, "Yeah, it's just my life. What's the big deal?"

One guy in particular paid a lot of attention. He didn't have anything good to say, but he was in the thick of the conversation. His name was Dave. About a week later Dave and a friend of his came knocking on my door at 3 in the morning. They apologized for waking me up. I told them it was no problem. Then he said, "I wanted to talk to you because I know we are going to hell and I thought you would know how to help." Usually the one that fights the most that is having the biggest inner struggle. That fighter is the one who is about to change. I have learned to watch for that. The one fighting you the hardest is the one who has been hurt, but is looking for a resolve. He is looking for an answer and a way out of his mess, but there is a battle inside for his soul so he is torn.

We talked and prayed until the sun came up. Dave was an alcoholic, but he was going to try to kick it. He had been a Christian until his fiancé left him. He fell... hard. He started drinking heavily, got into a lot of drugs, and became a heroin addict. He had kicked the heroin, which was amazing, but he was still an alcoholic. I saw Dave a lot. He lived right around the corner from me. He had a hard struggle, but the last I heard he was doing well. He had cleaned up and gotten his life back together. He always thanked me for helping him. He said that no one else would have talked to him like that in the middle of the night or put up with all the backsliding and relapses. I told him he would have done the same for me. At one point I wrote a song about Dave. It was called "My Soul, The Prize!" He loved it and so did everyone else. I used a funky tuning and weird chords. It is like the struggle that goes on inside all of us. The guy thinks it is just his thoughts, but really there are three voices: his, God's, and the devil's. The words are powerful and true:

"My Soul, The Prize!"

What am I doing? I know this is wrong,
At this time yesterday I thought I was strong.

Hang on child, no need to run.
Don't listen to him; you're missing all the fun!
My life is too short; I don't want to miss all the fun.
Haven't I taught you better? He only lies to kill.
Why do you even try? The mask you wear is a lie.

Chorus:

Fine, I fall. There's always tomorrow.
It's all a lie anyway. I'll drown my sorrow.
That's right you miserable wretch dance in the fire.
A little bit more will fulfill your desire.
What are you doing? Come back home please!

I'm sorry, I don't know what came over me.
Why do I do the things I hate?
Lean on me. I know this life is hard.
That may be fine for others, but you are far too scarred.
Is a little pleasure too much to ask for a heart that knows so much pain?
I carried my cross, you must do the same.
Go ahead indulge; you are not the one to blame.

Chorus:

Fine, I fall. There's always tomorrow.
It's all a lie anyway. I'll drown my sorrow.
That's right you miserable wretch dance in the fire.
A little bit more will fulfill your desire.
What are you doing? Come back home please!

Here I am, the same boat again,
Repenting of the same sins.
I rose to free from sin. Why won't you let me in?
Maybe you should take some time alone and think about this some more?
Maybe a little more time would be good,
After all Rome wasn't built in a day.

Now is the appointed time, today is the day of salvation.
Think of all you'll lose, it is worth damnation!

Chorus 2:

I fall on my knees. I run home to you.
It's something I've done before, but something I shouldn't do.
Come home son. I open my arms to you.
I love you so much I even died for you.
I leave now, but I'll be back.
When your soul sleeps, I'm on the attack!

Resolve:

All this time my soul the prize,
Two warriors fought, they fought for my life.
Voices inside my head, I thought they were mine.
Subtle hints, a battle was raging on inside,
Those on their knees, pleading to the King,
On my behalf won the victory, how could I have been so blind?
Jesus Christ, name above all names, no other saves,
My salvation, my strength, my song

Dave was just a good example of the struggle that goes on in this song. The truth is that we have all had the same experience to one degree or another. We may not have made it all the way to the end yet, but we are in there somewhere, struggling and wrestling, trying to find the truth. We are lost in the confusion of it all. We listen to the lies. We all feel the hopelessness. We all feel inadequate and alone at times. We all have this awful feeling inside that keeps us from trying. We feel that we are not good enough, that we won't measure up, and so we cease to try because we are afraid of failure. We all dream too small. We fall short because we don't really believe that we can conquer sin, but with Christ all things are possible! We can do anything and conquer everything with his help. "Can't" and "impossible" are two words that should never pass through our lips.

Over time we started to notice that the band and the Bible study were making a difference on campus and in town. It was very inspiring. In the meantime, I kept doing construction jobs. I learned more and more as time went on. I learned how to stick with a job and see it through no matter how hard it was or how difficult the people were to work for.

I learned to charge more money for my work. I talked to a fellow contractor who said he had been doing construction for over 10 years. He said the way he saw it he had a doctorate in construction and he should be paid for all his experience. That made sense to me, so I raised my prices again. I met a lot of interesting people and got to do some monumental things. I ended up working a lot of the guys in my band and some of the college students. They all learned something and made some money and I got helpers. It was good for everyone.

Remodeling actually takes a lot of vision, faith, endurance, strength, and patience. The homeowner doesn't know, or care for that matter, what you have to do to make their dream come true. They simply want something to be different and better. Of course they want to pay the least amount possible. They usually have champagne taste on a soda water salary. We have to look at the old house they have and know enough about the qualities of the structure to know what can and can't be done. My opinion is that "anything is possible with enough time and enough money." Which really is true. Every building out there was just a patch of dirt at one point. For someone to tell you that what you want to do is impossible is just lazy and ridiculous. If they say it will cost more than the house is worth than that might be true, but "impossible" isn't even an option.

We would come into people's homes and tear them up until it looked like they would never be fixed again. We had to protect what was good in the house like furniture and appliances and carpet, etc. It usually looked like a war zone for a while. We would bang around and make huge messes everywhere. We worked long, miserable hours. We got up early and stayed up late. We were always in the way and a tremendous inconvenience to the homeowner. We invaded their privacy. We knew all their secrets. We would see their dirt and imperfections. We would see how they really act around their family because eventually they get tired of faking it for the "hired help." We usually took away vital things from their living environment like electricity, water, kitchens, bathrooms, etc.

You could always tell when we were almost done with a job. The house looked terrible and the homeowners looked like they wanted to kill us. But then like magic, if you would just stick with it, the whole job would gel. We would clean up, get the tools out, polish everything up, and do finishing touches. All of the sudden we became heroes! We had done the impossible...again. The house looked better than ever. What was broken was now fixed. What leaked before now didn't. What was old was now new, and better than ever. The customers would smile from ear to ear and brag on their new house to all their friends.

It is interesting in retrospect that I did that for a living for so long. There are so many lessons to be learned there. Jesus was also a carpenter. A lot of us forget that. He knew how to build houses and furniture... and people. There are a lot of parallels between building or remodeling a house and fixing a broken person.

We are all broken. We want to think of ourselves as normal, which we all are. Normal people here and now have been broken at a young age. They have been hurt countless times. They feel alone even though people constantly surround them. A large percentage of normal people have been raped or molested (1 in 4). Almost all have issues with their parents in some way or another. Normal people feel hopeless, but are great at faking it. Normal people are amazing liars. We can deny that a problem exists for a lifetime even when it screams in our face everyday. We build cheap defense tactics to keep anyone away from our weaknesses, because we all have them...lots of them.

So, we can ignore a problem until it destroys us or we can call a carpenter to fix the issue. Just like remodeling a house it will hurt. You will have to give access to the things in your life that aren't pretty. There will be no more secrets, as if there ever were in the first place. Some things will have to be torn out and removed, but only for your good. Sometimes you will feel as if you are without essential things in life, but there is always an alternative that the carpenter has provided. He knows your needs, and is looking out for your best interests. And right when the mess is at its worst and you want to give up, then it all gels. It all comes together and you see the beauty of the whole thing. You see why He had to do it this way. It makes sense and you just want to show it off to all your friends. You want to try it out and brag about it.

The first person that needs to be remodeled is you, always. But once that is done, it is difficult to watch everyone else live in misery. Ever since I was sixteen years old all I wanted to do was sing from the rooftops what a great job God did remodeling my house inside. And so then I try to share that experience with other people. I wish we could just wave a magic wand across a broken house and it would be fixed, but we can't. I think that the same is true of broken people. We want to change in an instant, but it takes a lot of work, sweat, blood, tears, trial and error, repetitious failure sometimes, and persistence. I am privileged to have had the honor of helping so many people fix their homes. I am even more honored to have the blessing of helping so many people fix themselves. Obviously it isn't them or me. It is God. But God works through us if we let him. And to be an instrument of God like that is the most satisfying experience that I know of. Remodeling people is a hard job, but a glorious one.

One day I was by myself remodeling a home in Oklahoma City. I had a ladder propped up on the wall outside. I was inside at the time laying ceramic tile on the bathroom floor. I heard a low rumbling sound and a loud boom. At first I thought my ladder had slid down the side of the house and crashed, but then the foundation started to shake. I felt it in my knees because I was on my knees laying the floor. I got up and went outside. The ladder was still up. I didn't see anything, so I got up on the roof to see if something had happened up there. I saw smoke rising from about ten miles away. People started coming out of their homes. One of them said, "Can you see it?" I didn't have a clue what he was talking about. Then he told me they had just blown up the Federal Building. My first thought was "What is the Federal Building?" (I'm ignorant.) We were at least ten miles away and I not only heard the explosion, I felt it!

Lots of people I knew were hurt or killed and I knew lots of people that had loved ones in the building. We watched and knew lots of the people in the crowd at the funerals on TV. One of the ladies that went to my church was the last one out of the building for the Oklahoma Bombing. Timothy McVeigh honked at her from his Ryder truck and rudely told her to get out of the way. He came up and banged on her car window. He told her to move her car, but she was waiting for her husband who came out a moment later. They drove away and shortly after they left, the building blew up! She had to testify in court. She was one of the eyewitnesses that helped convict him. There was destruction everywhere. It was sad. Everyone joined together to help. Why do we only help each other when a tragedy occurs?

Back to the story. Months had gone by and I was getting comfortable with being single. The band was in some talent contest and I met a girl named Krista who I thought was attractive. So I asked her out. We went out to eat. Then I asked her out again. She said yes. Before I got the chance to actually go out with her again Lana showed back up and told me how sorry she was and that she wanted to get back together. I took her back. I went out to eat with Krista, but only to tell her that I was going out with Lana again. She told me that she had a boyfriend who lived out of town anyway. What a mess!

Lana was ready to get married and I had been for a long time, so I proposed...again. She insisted on getting yet another engagement ring and a wedding band, so I got them. Her parents tried to talk her out of it for a while. I'm sure they said terrible things about me. They still felt like I was a loser. They thought they would be supporting both of us for the rest of their lives. I was insulted. Finally, Lana stood up to them. She said, "We are getting married on May 20th. If you want to come you can. If not we are getting married anyway." I was proud of her. Her mother's tone changed instantly. All of the sudden she was like "What kind of wedding are you going to have? What kind of flowers? What kind of cake?"

Her dad was starting a concrete block factory in Denton, TX. and he needed someone to run it. So, we thought we would move to Denton for the summer. My band was pretty mad at me for that, but we went anyway. I moved right before school was out. I found us a small apartment that was only $350 a month. She moved her stuff down right before we got married and stayed in Arlington for a few days to get ready for the wedding while I worked in Denton.

Planning a wedding is stressful. I didn't even have to do anything. But it is the day every girl has waited for her whole life so you have to just smile and nod.

9 Set in Concrete

The day finally came. I had smashed my ring finger between two concrete blocks and it looked awful. I had a huge blood blister under my fingernail. When the whole thing started it was going to be very casual and inexpensive. Then her parents wanted to get her a nice dress, which led to a nice veil, which led to professional pictures, which led to flower arrangements, which led to nice cakes, which led to me being in a tuxedo. I wrote her a song and sang it at the wedding. My mom and grandfather flew in for the wedding. River was my best man and Jason was a groomsman.

I really didn't think that many people would show up. The place was full. It was surreal. By the end of it I didn't really feel any different than I did before. We were both like "That's it? **That** is the big deal? You just say a couple of lines in front of some people. Now we are married."

We got a lot of presents. It was a lot more than I expected, which was nothing from anyone. We went to a hotel for a couple days and made up for lost time. It was great to introduce her as my "wife" now. We spent money on frivolous stuff just because it was our honeymoon and we could. It was a lot of fun.

We got married on Friday, May 20th, 1995. There was a guy that we both went to church with named Al who was at our wedding. I shook his hand and we laughed and talked that day. The next day his daughter graduated and he celebrated that. The day after that he died. We went to the funeral while we were on our honeymoon. It was sad. Death is a weird thing. You can be talking to someone one day and thinking nothing of it. Nothing special or unusual happens and then **BANG** they are gone, never to return... here anyway. Open casket funerals are always weird too because they always look so fake lying there.

I always cry at funerals. I don't cry because I feel sorry for the person in the coffin. I cry for their families that they leave behind that will never really heal. And I cry because I know one day it will be me in that box. Don't think for a second that that makes me sad. They are tears of joy and hope. One day I will be home. One day I will leave this place of pain and brokenness. One day I will see Jesus face to face. One day I can thank Him for everything he has done for me. One day I won't be tempted anymore. I will be done with the race, the struggle, and the fight. One day, I too, will come home to my reward!

A long time ago I came to grips with the fact that I will surely die one day. We all will. As I am now I can't enter into glory. My very presence in paradise would poison it. I am unworthy. For a tree to be all it can be the seed must die to itself so it can be much more than just a seed. I too will die to myself so that I can be so much more. I cry at funerals because no matter how good my life is here, I am always jealous of the person in the box. I remember one morning I woke up in Washington when I was 18 years old and I noticed my heart beating. I know that seems trivial, but I thought, "This thing in my chest hasn't skipped a beat my whole life. One day though, it will stop beating... forever." I wrote this song:

This Lonely Heart

One day this lonely heart will beat no more,
Oh what a happy and glorious morn',
For though my body has met the greatest pain on earth,
And to death I have fallen,
My soul is now with the Lord and I am now in heaven,

My time on earth is over; the veil has been lifted,
The two who were divided now meet,
My Lord and I, we talk face to face,
He says my son was that such a feat?

For we have forever, you are mine and I am yours,
And by the way "Well done with your chores",
I know it wasn't easy, but was it really hard?
After all I was with you all the while

I ended up going back to work early because my father-in-law needed me. Working for him was as fun as flossing with sandpaper. I would get up at the crack of dawn and drive 30 minutes to get to the plant. I ran it so I had to be the first to get there and I was the last to leave. It was pretty ghetto. There was a gravel parking lot with a small building on it. He kept some equipment in the building and a phone. It leaked and was rat-infested and stinky.

There were a few thousand plastic forms for these concrete blocks stacked on pallets. There was a washbasin that we poured diesel in. We had drilled a hole in the bottom of the tank and hooked a pump up to it. The pump went right up above to a few sprayers that would spray the diesel on the forms (diesel lubricates the forms so that when you take the concrete out it doesn't stick to the form as much.) So, one guy would stand there pushing forms through this diesel sprayer we rigged up. It was always clogging and messing up somehow. He would push the forms to the next guy.

There was a ramp that we made out of some railroad ties and gravel. Concrete trucks would back up onto the ramp and pour their concrete into a makeshift funnel we had made out of some old iron. There was a lever that would open and close the chute at the bottom of our funnel-thing. It never worked right, ever. So guy number two had to grab the form from guy number one and shake this funnel contraption until enough concrete poured into it to fill the form. Then he passed it to guy number three who would get a stick and scrape off the excess concrete.

Guys four and five would then stack the heavy concrete that was now in forms onto pallets. Then I had to jump on the forklift and move the full pallets to a drying area. We did 3 full trucks a day. In between trucks we had to break the concrete out of the forms that had been sitting around for a few days. We had these loud, obnoxious vibrator machines that we had to slam the forms on and then hit the back of them with rubber mallets and then stack them down. Then we had to shrink-wrap them and stack them in another place until the eighteen-wheelers would come and then I would load them on the eighteen-wheelers and they would go to the job sites. I also had to constantly re-grade the parking lot and clean all the machinery. All that concrete was messy!

I did the math once. Every guy out there lifted about 250,000 pounds of concrete a day... by hand! I was the boss, which meant I actually lifted more than anyone else. We used temporary labor since nobody in their right mind would ever want to do a job like that for more than a day. They would have the option of coming back the next day, which almost never happened. What that meant was that I got to train a brand new crew every single day. What fun. This would have been a hard enough job with intelligent individuals, but of course I was dealing with the bottom feeders and the underachievers in the world.

These were truly the least dependable people on the face of the earth. They were only late every single day... that is if they showed up at all. There were times I had to do entire truck pours completely by myself. That is a lot of work. The concrete truck drivers would just watch me running around trying to do everything alone. Then they would get impatient, like "Would you hurry up?" They gave me a hard time every day. It was so frustrating.

My workers were mostly homeless people from Dallas. They made minimum wage, but we paid twice that for them. They had to pay for their ride out there. They paid for their gloves and boots. They paid for the ride home. Then they stayed in the shelter at the temp service, which cost them more money. By the end of the day they would make about $30. I couldn't really blame them for being lazy. I wouldn't do all that work for $30 a day. It was sad to hear them talk. Most of them were criminals. Some were rapists and murderers. Almost all of them were alcoholics and drug addicts.

They would always talk about what they were going to do that night with the money they had made that day. Those conversations mostly consisted of a lot of drinking and drugs. Everyday I had a new crew and everyday they had the exact same conversations. I would spend our breaks and lunches trying to inspire them and encourage them in whatever way I could. Sometimes I would break through a little. It was hard when I knew I would only see each of them for one day. I heard a story about a girl on the beach. Thousands of starfish had washed ashore and were dying. She ran frantically back and forth throwing them back in the water. A man saw her and he stopped her. He said "Little girl, why do you even bother trying? You will never get them all back in the water. Why don't you just give up?" She paused for a moment. She looked down at the one dying at her feet, picked it up, threw it back in the water, and said, "You are right. I will never get them all back in the water, but I bet that one appreciates it." Then she went back to the job at hand which was saving the helpless.

I don't know if I ever made a difference to any of those guys, but I hope I did. I often pray for my friends and family. I try to communicate the gospel to them, but sometimes they just don't listen. So, I pray that someone else will come into their lives and translate the gospel in a way that I couldn't and that their eyes could be opened. I know that there are other people praying the same thing for people that I meet everyday. I also know that the workers are few.

So, I try to remember that EVERYONE I meet has some loved one praying for them. Perhaps I can be an answer to the prayers of their loved ones. So, I try to do my part. I try to set a good example and always be attentive to what **isn't** said. People are fragile and you never really know how much of a difference you make in some stranger's life. I know lots of strangers have made a difference in my life. So, I want to do the same. The task at hand is never as important as the person doing it. If there is someone hurting on my crew I will make it a priority to meet that need and then deal with whatever work needs to be done.

I got to talk to a lot of guys at that plant. A lot of hard-working guys that were down on their luck and were being taking advantage. Granted, they had made some bad choices, but we all have. Sometimes they would stick around for a few weeks. I stuck around for 6 months, which was about 6 months too long!

There would be times when I had to work on other jobs. We did erosion control. So, we were always working with heavy machinery and dirt. We used backhoes, track hoes, loaders, bulldozers, tampers, forklifts, sky tracks, and trenchers. I got to learn how to use them all since I was the foreman. We were always working in some creek bed or river or lake trying to redirect water and stop erosion, which is a lot harder then it sounds. It is also very expensive. I learned a lot about big numbers working for Bill. Him and his partner would be talking about spending millions of dollars as if it were nothing. They couldn't be bothered with petty cash like a few thousand dollars here or there.

I also saw how easily you could make millions of dollars and blow it all on poor management and lack of quality control. There was always money moving but there was never a profit! It baffled me, but I learned from the experience.

I will give you a few examples of what a day was like working erosion control. One day we were neck deep in a river with rakes. It was over a hundred degrees outside. They would dump a bunch of gravel in the water with a track hoe. We had to hold our breath and then go under water and rake the gravel into the right places all day. At one point I came up for air and looked and there was a snake swimming right towards me. He is in snake heaven now.

Another time we were on the job and I got poison ivy all over my body. And I was covered in mosquito bites and chiggers and a black widow bit me on the shin. That was all in the same day! I was an itch fest. I had to get some antibiotics for the spider bite. I looked like Job from the Bible. I still worked. I wouldn't stop working for anything.

So, one day I was waiting for a concrete truck to come. I was waiting for my workers to come. I had done everything around the plant that could be done. I was sitting on a huge pile of broken blocks waiting. I wrote this song:

Feeding Frenzy

Feeding frenzy with poisoned food,
Smile as I backstab you,
Run, run, fast as you can't, you can not catch me,
I am but a dream, I am but a dream, I am but a dream
Pleasure Island is a game,
See who wins fortune and fame,
To win you sin, and to sin you lose,
I mock you, I mock you, I mock you

Run, Kill, Steal,
Forsake all to have my fill, alone I die,
Naked as I came!

Tension builds, I'm too busy to care,
My riches fly away like chaff in the air,
I kill to reach the top of greed,

It hasn't fulfilled a single need.
Not one single need, I feel hollow inside,
I feel like dying, but I've already died!
At the top of the bottom, I cry alone,
The more I have the more I need,
But still I run.
Still I run, perhaps in vain?
Agony within, I must win this game!

Run, Kill, Steal,
Forsake all to have my fill, alone I die,
Naked as I came!

     I was ready to move on from this job. I talked with Bill. The plant wasn't making money like he wanted it to. He asked how long I thought it would take me to get back into construction. I told him it wouldn't take long. He had heard that you could make money by buying junk houses and fixing them up and selling them. He asked if I wanted to do that. I agreed to look into it as soon as Lana and I got back from a belated honeymoon.

     I had saved about $7,000 and so I took a month off of work. Lana didn't work. We drove with no set schedule or time to be back. We saw the entire western half of America and we stopped at every tourist site we could find. We went from Texas to New Mexico. We saw the Painted Desert and the Petrified Forest, which was more like the petrified log. We went to Arizona and saw the Grand Canyon. Pictures can't do it justice. It is breathtaking, truly.

     We went to Nevada and then to California. We saw the Golden Gate Bridge, Los Angeles, San Francisco, and Sacramento. We went to the beaches and swam. We saw all kinds of things. We saw a huge herd of seals. That was pretty cool. We visited places that I had been when I was younger. Then we drove to Quincy, California to see Kyle, my college roommate. We stayed there a few days and visited.

Lana had been trying to track down my birth father in her spare time. Not having a dad never bothered me, but she seemed to want to find him. Kyle's dad was a cop and he told us off the record that my dad had lived in Eureka and Arcada, California. So, we drove to the northern coast of California and found the towns. We asked around and got a few leads, but we never found him.

We drove up through the Redwood Forrest, another breathtaking sight. We went up through Oregon and then went to TomFest, which was a big Christian festival. River was up there. So we met him and James. We stayed there for several days. It was a lot of fun. We went swimming in the lake and camped out the whole time. We actually camped out for most of that trip.

Then we drove to Seattle. We found another friend from college and drove to his house. We stayed there for a few days. His parents needed their bathrooms remodeled so I did it while I was there. I made a couple hundred dollars and they got two new bathrooms. We went through Canada. Then we drove to Republic and visited everyone up there. I saw Phyllis and Jamie and Jeff and everyone else up there. I gave Lana a tour of the goldmine and the sawmill.

Then we visited my mother and my brother Chris and Bill (my mother's husband). We stayed for several days. We drove to NNC and saw some old friends. There were only a few left. We went through Montana over to Wyoming and went through Yellowstone and the Grand Tetons. We drove south through Utah and Colorado and back across to Oklahoma to visit some friends at SNU. Then we drove home. We had a lot of fun. That is the longest period of time in my life since I was 15 years old that I haven't worked. It was very nice. We did everything we wanted to do. We saw everything we wanted to see. Then we decided to move back to Arlington, Texas.

I found a HUD home and Bill said he would back me on buying it. He would supply the money and I would do the work and we would split the profit. I put an offer in on it and put down some of my own earnest money because time was of the essence. I got the house and then Bill backed out.

So, I had to find an investor to buy the house from me, quick! It wasn't a great move on his part, but I made the best of it. I found someone to buy it. I went to close on this house with no money at all. I sat down at a table and bought the house with some other lady's money. I closed on it and then we passed the paperwork down the table. She was buying it with someone else's money also. So she closed on the house and then they passed the papers down one last time. The last guy was using his own money so he actually got the house. I made $1,500. She made about $3,000 and the guy got the house. I'm sure he just fixed it and sold it right away.

Then I found another house. They only wanted $25,000 for it. I offered them $10,000. We agreed on $15,000. I got a loan and bought the house. It was condemned. The roof had holes; the floor had holes and was rotted. The plumbing didn't work. There was no electricity or gas. There were holes in all the walls, but we loved it. We moved all of our stuff into Lana's parents garage and moved into her old bedroom for 6 weeks or so.

Her parents didn't like that at all. They told everyone that I was a loser and that they were going to have to support us for the rest of their lives and now here we had moved in with them. To top it off they didn't like us sleeping in the same room, but we were married so we did anyway. Right after we bought the house Lana got pregnant. That added fuel to the fire for them.

I worked night and day to get that house fixed. As usual, nobody believed I could do it. They all thought it was too big a task for me and that I would fail and go bankrupt. I almost tripled the size of the house. It was 700 square feet before and I made it 1880 square feet. I added a second story. I put in a corner Jacuzzi bathtub with two faucets in the shower. We had custom tile. We had hardwood floors everywhere. There were skylights and there was recessed lighting in every room. We had custom cabinets that I made myself. I rewired the entire house and did all new plumbing, gas, and phone lines. I put in a satellite system and huge walk-in closets. There was an 800 square foot deck and a tool shed in the back. It wasn't a mansion, but we did it. We did it quickly and inexpensively. The total cost of the house was $40,000 with all the remodeling. It seemed like a lot of money to me at the time, but it was really very cheap for all that we got.

We moved in as soon as we closed on the house and we moved out of her parent's house. Everyone was amazed that we had done it. The Bible says that faith without action is dead, like the body without the soul. I have always been a firm believer in putting my faith into action. I believed we could do it. We counted the cost and then we did it. Most people just want to sit around and talk about how they could do something, but they never actually do it. I am not that guy! I say it and the next time you look, it is already done! Faith in action is powerful. Try it.

As soon as I finished the house I already had jobs waiting for me. Everyone wanted to get me to fix something of theirs. After all, if I could do all that, I could certainly fix their little problem, right? I started doing a lot of jobs. Since I had been out of the state for a year or so River had gotten a job answering phones for a television evangelist. He had also gotten married to his wife, Kishta, who also worked there. It just so happens that they needed to remodel a huge building and they wanted an individual to do the work instead of a company so it would be cheaper for them. I looked at the job.

10 Affordable Dreams

By this time I had done a lot of different kinds of work so I was fairly confident, but I'll have to admit the job at hand looked a little overwhelming to me. The building was about 20,000 square feet. It was a two story commercial building. They had blue prints and architects and engineers that needed everything to be exactly to specks. There were a lot of things we had to install that I was unfamiliar with at the time. We had to install a dumbwaiter, which is like a mini-elevator. I had never done that before! We had to make a safe room with all kinds of tripwires and safeguards in the walls. We had to make a computer room with a raised floor. The room had to be airtight because it had a halon gas fire safety system. I wasn't sure I could do it all, but I simply smiled and said, "Yes, we can do all that."

They wanted to pay me hourly so I got $26 an hour and my guys got $8 an hour. I hired some friends of mine and we all got to work. Every other day something on the blueprints changed. We never had the proper resources or authority to just get the job done so it took longer than expected. We were on that job for 8 months. I did other jobs in the meantime, but that is still way too long for me to be doing one thing. I learned a lot, as usual.

One of the things I learned is that there is a big myth among contractors. We seem to think that if the job is bigger than we can afford to cut the price per unit since there will be more work. The thought is that our costs stay basically the same for labor and tools, but we can make more money since the big number is higher. The truth is that there are increased expenses and liability, so the cost per unit should stay the same. If there isn't enough money in the job to make it worth while then let it go. There will be other jobs.

I also learned how to ask for huge orders and huge amounts of money without blinking an eye. That sounds easy, but most people can't do it with confidence. When you are building something that costs several hundred thousand or several million dollars than you have to get the resources you need to do such a thing or else it is time to move on. I learned how to argue with people that had a lot more than I did and I learned to shut up when it wasn't worth the fight. I learned how to run a big crew. I learned how to delegate instead of doing everything myself all the time. I learned that a good leader leads by example, not by force.

My guys knew that I wouldn't ask them to do anything that I wouldn't do myself, and that I always had their safety and best interests at heart. I also learned by watching some of the sub-contractors on that job that you don't have to be anything special to do big jobs. I am convinced that I could pay a few hundred dollars to put an ad in the yellow pages for ANY service in the world. I could have no training, no credentials, no experience, and no references and I could get work right away doing whatever I choose to do.

Look around you right now. See all the little things? See the toothpicks, or the screws that hold something together, or the shoes on your feet, or the CD you are listening to, or the chair you are sitting in? Every little thing has a crew of people that put them together and sell them. The guy that actually made the toothpick or the screw is barely scraping by. The guy that owns the company that made these things is rich! Working doesn't make you money. Money makes you money! So, how do you make money if you don't have it? How do you make money if you weren't born with it? If you were like most people and didn't have a perfect life with a huge trust fund... then how do you get ahead?

If you had the choice to work for one month and you could either make $100 an hour with all the over time you wanted, OR you could work the same month, 31 days, and on your first day you would make a penny, on the second day that penny would double, on the third day that would double and so on for thirty one days. Which would you choose? Obviously, it won't be laid out for you like that in real life. If you choose the $100 an hour and work really hard, let's say 100 hours a week for 4 and a half weeks then you make pretty good money. It works out like this:

40 hours a week at $100 an hour equals $4,000 straight pay
PLUS
60 hours a week at $150 an hour (overtime) equals $9,000
Times 4.5 weeks is $13,000 x 4.5 equals $58,500

Now there aren't many people who would turn down sixty grand for a month's worth of work even if you did have to work 100 hours a week for a month, but what if you took the penny?

Day 1: one cent
Day 2: 2 cents
Day 3: 4 cents
Day 4: 8 cents
Day 5: 16 cents
Day 6: 32 cents
Day 7: 64 cents

Week one seems sad at best. Most people give up here. They aren't getting the payoff they expected. They are unappreciated and underpaid. That is way less than minimum wage! But, stick around for a little while and watch what happens.

Day 8: $1.28
Day 9: $2.56
Day 10: $5.12
Day 11: $10.24
Day 12: $20.48
Day 13: $40.96
Day 14: $81.92

You know what, maybe I was wrong to think this could work. It is a lot better than last week, but look around. Fast food workers are making more money!

Day 15: $163.84
Day 16: $327.68
Day 17: $655.36
Day 18: $1,310.72
Day 19: $2,621.44
Day 20: $5,242.88
Day 21: $10,485.76

Well, that's finally something. But, you have worked for 3 weeks and made less than if you had worked for one week the other way.

Day 22: $20,971.52
Day 23: $41,943.04
Day 24: $83,886.08
Day 25: $167,772.16
Day 26: $335,544.32
Day 27: $671,088.64
Day 28: $1,342,177.28

Oh wow! I mean what else can you say?

Day 29: $2,684,354.46
Day 30: $5,368,708.82
Day 31: $10,737,417.64

Pretty impressive, huh? I'd do that. I know you are thinking no one will give you that opportunity. And you are right. No one probably will. The truth is that you can work for an individual or a company for 40 years and you will never make that kind of money. The guy at the top is the guy with the money. He took the risk. He made the investment. He assumes responsibility if it fails. So, he gets the reward if he sticks with it. The owner will always keep the profit and so he should. You would if it was your company, wouldn't you? Even if you make a lot of money working for someone else it is only because you are making them more money. If you weren't, they would get rid of you.

If you want to live like everyone else, then please do. Enjoy your life, watch TV, watch your kids grow, and enjoy weekends and holidays. But don't kid yourself into thinking you will one day win the lottery and it will all be good for you. Don't get me wrong there is a lot of contentment in being middle class or even in being poor. You can sleep at night. When you leave work, you don't have to think about it any more until you get there again. Life is a lot simpler. I think if I had it to do over again I wouldn't have chosen to chase money. It is never enough. Regardless of what I would do now, I am writing about what I actually did.

I always wanted to be something more. My mother told me that when I was about 4 years old that I was in a cardboard box in the floorboard of our old beater of a car with River and Ann in the box with me. I looked up at her and I said "This being poor thing might be fun for you, but I am going to be rich when I grow up." I don't remember actually saying that. My mom told me later after I had made some money. I didn't really care about the things money could buy. I just didn't want to be poor. I always hated bills that were late and making excuses and borrowing money from people. I just wanted to be able to live in peace without worrying about money. I have never cared what kind of car I drove or what kind of house I lived in or what kind of clothes I wore or what kind of food I ate. I just wanted to have my needs covered.

After the television evangelist job I got a new plan. Up until that time I had always just said " I'll do this one thing and then after that I'll get a real job." I had been saying that for years when I finally realized I am making a pretty good living off of this. **Maybe this is a real job?** Maybe Doug was right and this would one day turn into a profitable company for me. Maybe if I stuck with it long enough my penny would double until I was a millionaire. I thought if I could just save one million dollars I could live off the interest for the rest of my life. Then I wouldn't have to work any more and I could be with my family all the time.

I still owed money on the house I had built. I figured that I would pay off the house and then start saving money until I reached a million dollars and then I would retire by the time I was thirty. Everyone thought it was impossible. Everyone thought I was an idiot for even believing such a foolish thing. Maybe I was, but I did the math and it worked out so I tried. I made a plan to pay off large amounts of money on the principal part of my loan instead of just interest.

Did you know that if you make minimum payments on your home on a standard 30 year loan that you will pay 3 and a half times the original value of your house? It is true. Look at your amortization chart. If you make one extra payment per year you will knock 15 years off of your loan. If you double your payments you will pay it off in 5 years. If you triple your payments you will pay off in 4 years, and if you quadruple you will pay off in 3 years. I paid off my house in 3 years and 3 months! They said it couldn't be done, but while they were talking about all the reasons it couldn't be done, I just did it! You can do anything you set your mind to. Make a plan, do the math, stick with it, and it will pay off. Forty percent of homeowners own their homes outright? They don't owe anyone anything. It is theirs. Granted, most of them are older, but I joined their ranks at age 25! Don't tell me I can't do something!

Back to the story. I was very fast at construction and so I could do it for a fair price. I wasn't afraid to do anything, so we could basically do everything that anyone wanted. Everything I did was custom so I didn't charge extra for custom work. I really enjoyed making people's dreams come true. I was a problem solver. If there was a way to do something I would find it for them and I would help them find a way to pay for it.

There is always money if you know where to look for it. One night I was laying in bed talking to my wife about what we did for people and I said, "I make people's dreams come true for an affordable price. It is very satisfying. I feel like I have made their homes better and their lives better. Wow, that is a cool name. Affordable Dreams. Affordable Dreams Construction, I like that." And so it was born. I got a DBA as John Tunnell *Doing Business As* Affordable Dreams Construction for $11 at the courthouse and it was official.

Speaking of being born, while all this was happening my daughter was born. I had never had medical insurance and Lana's pregnancy was kind of a surprise to us so we started looking into alternatives to having our baby in a hospital. I mentioned that I had been born at home. We talked to my mother and then we found a mid-wife. It was a lot cheaper and really better in a lot of ways. Lana was a trooper. She was in labor for 11 hours. She had Lily at home in our bedroom with no medication and she only cried out once. I was proud of her.

It is a helpless feeling to see someone you love in pain and not really be able to do anything to help except tell her it will be ok soon (you hope?). Lily Joy Tunnell was born on July 28th, 1996. I got to help deliver her into this world. I got to cut the cord. It was an amazing experience, a little scary, but amazing none the less. She was so beautiful! She was so tiny and perfect. Her fingers were so small and delicate. Children are miracles. All of the sudden you get a real life object lesson of how God must love us. Once you have kids you realize that there is really nothing they can do to make you stop loving them. Even if they are really bad, you still love them. If they keep you up all night, or crap on you, or throw up on you, if they break things, or cost a lot of money it still doesn't matter. You come running if you hear them cry. Of course they will mess up. They are babies. Of course they will do things that are wrong. Of course they will be selfish and shortsighted. Of course they won't understand the big picture, but you don't love them any less.

It takes years for a child to grow into an adult, but you love them every step of the way. And then it makes sense how God can love us even though we are imperfect and we fall. All of the sudden you realize that we are all just children in the sight of God. Even if we get to be 100 years old we are still just children to Him, but we are His children! And He loves us, not because of what we can do for Him. He loves us just because.

Having children is also a huge responsibility. They are always on your mind. As the sole breadwinner in the house I felt a tremendous responsibility to hurry up and make my money so I could retire and be with my family. I figured Lily wouldn't remember being an infant anyway; so I could work real hard now and then spend time with her later when she could remember.

Lana was a great mother. She did so much research into every possible technique of childrearing and nutrition it was unbelievable. She was always thinking of Lily's welfare. She was good at that. I was not. I was good at making money. I wasn't a bad father, but I guess I wasn't as good of a father as I could have been. I regret that a lot. In all fairness to me I was under a great deal of stress and I had more responsibility than almost anyone I knew my age. I had grown the company quite a bit.

When Lily was fourteen months old I got a card to the "Best Dad in the World", which apparently was me. Inside was a positive pregnancy test. We wanted Lily to have a friend to grow up with, so nine months later Benjamin William Tunnell was born in the second bedroom of our house. We used a midwife again and Ben came out much easier. Once again Lana was a trooper. And once again she was a great mother. And once again I ended up feeling overwhelmed and ended up working even more. Ben was born on May 8th, 1998. Both of my children look exactly like me. They are fun, cute, smart, innocent, loving, forgiving, and full of energy. I love them more than words can say.

I worked a lot, but all of my free time was spent with my family. We had a lot of fun. I think I feel worse about my qualities as a dad because of the way that Lana talked to me all the time. Nothing I ever did was good enough for her. We had more money and financial freedom than anyone I knew, especially as young as we were. I never hit her or the kids. I didn't drink, smoke, do drugs, cuss, or sleep around. I never raised my voice to them. I always tried my very best to be the best father and husband I could be, but I guess it wasn't good enough for her. Kids don't know the difference. You are their dad and they love you no matter what. I love that about kids. If only adults could learn to be as forgiving and innocent as children the world would be a lot better place. Why does everyone always have to be so hard on each other?

Everyone thinks that their kids are the best kids in the world. So, I won't bore you with all the details of what my children did at every single stage of their lives. I love them very much and think they are the best kids in the world. We did all the normal kid and dad things. So just fill in the blanks for yourself, unless we talk in person one day.

Every year Affordable Dreams grossed lots of money, but somehow it never netted out that much. Every year I got just a little bit more tired of listening to whiny women complain about the smallest details as if they were monumental. Every year I got a little more jaded by people who didn't pay for work that I had done in good faith. I got tired of people lying and stopping payments on checks. I got tired of working over a hundred hours a week for a lot of thankless people who wanted something for nothing. SO, every year I would raise my prices. My thought was that I would get less work, but make more money per job. The exact opposite happened every time. Every time I would raise my prices I would get more work, I would get more respect, I would have less hassle, and more referrals. It was so crazy!

I would think that I could spend more time at home with my family if I just raised my prices. I thought I would scare away customers and I didn't really care if I did. But people want someone who believes in himself. People want someone who is confident that the price they are giving is the lowest price possible... if you care about quality at all. People want to know that there are no hidden costs because you were just upfront with them from the beginning instead of selling a job at a low price and then raising the price later. So every year our numbers doubled. It was just like the penny doubling. You work hard for a long time for what seems like nothing and no reward and then if you stick with it, it pays off.

I paid off my house like I already said. I started saving all the extra money. I worked all the time so I didn't have time to spend it except on business expenses. I wanted to get out of customer service so I started buying junk houses with the extra money I had saved. I got a line of credit from the bank for $35,000 and I used that as a cushion financially in between buying a house and selling it. I also got a business credit card because the amount of cash I was carrying with me every day was getting ridiculous. They gave me a $20,000 limit on my credit card. I got frequent flyer miles on the card so I would get a free trip every $20,000 I spent on the card. I would pay it off at the end of every month so I never paid interest. I have flown to a lot of places for free.

I bought a house that had a huge fire in it for $24,000. I just treated it like it was any other job. We went in and remodeled everything. By the time we were done the original owners bought it back from me for $62,000. They said they loved the house and it was the best house they could get for the price. Plus, we did it so fast they never had to change their address. I had some expenses in the house so I didn't actually clear all that much money, but it is still a nice feeling to get a check that big with your name on it!

After that, I bought a house for $34,000. It wasn't as bad as the burned house, but it was still disgusting! It got nicknamed the "Egg Sandwich House". We had nicknames for a lot of the jobs we did. It helped us remember them and it was funny to laugh about. Mark was one of the guys who worked for me. He went to look at the house with me before I bought it. It stunk! There was trash everywhere. It was unlivable, but there were people living in it.

While we were walking through the house and trying to act professional about the horrible living conditions in there, a fat two year old kid came around the corner. He was eating an egg sandwich. Part of it fell on the filthy floor. He didn't skip a beat. He reached down and ate it. We were pretty grossed out by it, so later we called it "the egg sandwich house". It fit so well. It was so disgusting!

Anyway, we got it all cleaned up and fixed everything in it. I sold it for $63,000. It is so nasty cleaning a place like that, but knowing there is hope and a payoff at the end will keep you going. People are the same way. I look at the filthiest, most vile people and I know God can make them "the nicest one on the block"... with a little work. That is what He does. He takes that which is broken and makes everything new. Behold the old is gone. It is now a new creation. You wouldn't even recognize the finished product from the original. That is what He has done for me.

Jesus never condemned anyone for being a sinner? He never accused the prostitute or the tax collector or the drunk or the thief. He never even addressed the fact that they had done any of that stuff. They already knew. Everyone knew. It went without saying. He looked at the woman who had been caught in adultery and simply said "Woman where are your accusers? Has no one condemned you? Then neither do I condemn you...Go now and leave your life of sin."
- John 8:11

He never denies the fact that we are in sin, nor does he simply dismiss it as if we will be all right if we keep going the direction we are going. But He never seems to bring it up either. He looks on us with compassion and says, "I can fix that if you will let me." The question is will we let Him fix us? Do we believe He can? Does He own us yet? Is there enough evidence to convince us that He has dealt with someone as bad as us and succeeded? Yes, He has and yes He can, but will YOU let Him? You could be the best one on the block, or the neighborhood. It will take some work. Are you willing to go through the remodeling? It is a little painful at times. Sometimes you feel like everything is hopeless, but that is right when everything is about to come together. Stick with God and He will see you through. It is worth it.

Every year our numbers doubled for Affordable Dreams Construction. I was well on my way to reaching my retirement goal of saving a million dollars by the time I was thirty years old. We were right in the middle of an extended economic boom. In fact, it was the biggest construction boom in recorded history. Everyone was talking about it. Money was flowing like water. The company was making about $15,000 a week. If you wanted us to do a job for you, you would have to wait for a few days for me to even call you back. This was before cell phones. Then it would be about 6 weeks until I could look at the job to even give you a price. Then it would be about 4 months until I could get to it. That wasn't because we were lazy. We were just that busy! I was working well over 100 hours a week.

In 2000 I estimated that the company should gross about $750,000 and the next year we could get closer to $1,000,000! It wouldn't be long now. I could spend time with my family and do what I wanted to do. Half way through the year we were right on schedule. We had grossed around $400,000. We might even beat my goal. Then for no reason at all I started asking the people around me some important questions. At first it was just curiosity. I was thinking I could retire soon and so I wanted to know what other people dreamed of. I wanted to be well informed and have a plan based on sound advice and well-rounded council. I just wanted to do some cool things that I had been missing out on since I worked so much.

Here are the questions I asked:

1) What would you change about your life if you knew for a fact that you would die tomorrow at this time? If you are in school, would you still go? If you worked, would you go to work on the last day of your life? Would you make peace with your enemies? Would you tell your family that you loved them? Would you make peace with God? Would you ask for forgiveness or would you let your heart stay hard? Is there anything you would want to squeeze out of your last day of life that you haven't done yet? What would you do?

2) What if you had a week to live? What other things could you do in a week? Would you get your house in order? Would you make a will? Would you tie up loose ends? Would you make a last chance attempt at something you believe in? Would you beg for your life? Would you bargain and grovel? Or would you be at peace? Would you be proud or ashamed of the life you have lived? When you have to give an account for your life in just one week, is there anything you would try to do to make it right while you still had the chance?

3) What if you had exactly one year until you died? That is enough time to get everything that is undone in your life in order. It is even enough time to make a change that is legitimate and maybe even make a difference. So, what would you do? Would you be fearless? Would you go skydiving or bungee jumping or scuba diving? Would you cherish every moment, knowing all the while that you were living on borrowed time?

4) Finally, what would you do if you knew for a fact that you had 5 years to live? If there was no question. It wasn't the way we think now where it could be today or it could be 80 years. What if you knew you had exactly 5 years? In five years you could change the world if you tried hard enough. You could leave a permanent mark. You could be remembered forever. It might not be in your time or on your terms or even in your lifetime, but if you tried hard enough you could do it. So, what is it that you believe in enough to live and die for? What do you feel so passionately about that you would sacrifice everything for it? Is there anything like that for you? Anything at all?

The answers I got were so disheartening that I could hardly stand it. Almost everyone wanted to get as many loans as possible since they wouldn't have to pay them back because they would be dead already. They all wanted to party. It was almost all selfish wants and ambitions. It was all emptiness. Sadder than that was the fact that not one person, not even one, was doing what they wanted to do with their life! We had all just let life happen to us. We had made excuses. We had gone astray. We had lost our first love! We had all "grown up". So, I asked more people because I thought that maybe it was just in my circle of influence that hopelessness reined. I found that life is what happens while we are making plans. The amazing thing is that we remain blind to our own shortcomings.

So then I turned the questions on myself. What was at first casual curiosity became deep self-exploration. What would I do? What **will** I do? All I ever wanted to do was help people and put a smile on God's face. Is that really what I was doing? I mean I wasn't bad. I meant well. I was honest. I worked hard. I did all the right things and avoided all the wrong things. I was disciplined. I was talented and I was using the talents I had to do the best job possible. I had tried to get a job as a missionary and as a pastor. They wouldn't take me. I did share my faith all the time with my employees and my customers. I tried to set a good example. I tried to be a good father and husband. I tried to keep my life balanced.

But, had I missed the mark? Was I just like everyone else? Did I want to be remembered as a man who could fix homes and who made a lot of money? Was that really all I wanted to be? And what if it didn't happen the way I planned? What if it took another ten years before I could retire? What if I became spoiled with all the money and couldn't live without spending thousands of dollars a week? Had I become what I hated?

And then I thought further. What can I do? How can I make a difference? Not in another world or another lifetime, not if I were born a king or if I were rich and powerful, but what can I do right here and now with the resources that I have? What can I, John Tunnell, do as a 27-year-old husband and father of two with limited resources and limited talents? What do I even want to do? I was tired of doing service work. I didn't want to break my back for money anymore. I was already feeling the pain of that. I had about two years where I couldn't feel the back of my legs or my lower back. They were just numb. I still worked, but it was only by pure will power. I didn't want to do sales. I was good at it, but I was tired of pleasing customers. They can be so petty and cruel. Even the nicest people will stab you in the back and verbally abuse you if it will save them a few dollars.

I want to interject here and say why not just be kind to the people who work for you? Tip your waitress. She only makes $2.13 an hour. Remember her name, she remembers yours. The guys putting your roof on will work ten times harder for you if you make then something to drink or buy them lunch. It is hot up there, and it is hard work! The guy working on your car will be less likely to take advantage of you if are polite to him and treat him like a professional. He knows things about your car that you can't even pronounce. If you don't think that service people deserve your money, then go and do it yourself. First of all, you probably can't. But even if you can, you don't. So pay them and be nice. You will be happier. They will be happier. You will have better service. And the blessing will pass on to others until it comes back to you again... just when you need it the most.

I didn't know anything about computers. I didn't want to go back to school. I didn't have a degree. I didn't want to manufacture anything. I have done that and it is hard work. I didn't want to sit in an office and die inside. I didn't want to manage something for someone else. Being self-employed will spoil you. You make your own rules and your own hours. Granted that translates to the fact that you work all the time and answer to everyone, but you still know that the final decision is yours. I thought long and hard. I had a family to support. I had to make money somehow, but I wanted it to be something worthwhile. If it was any of the stuff I just mentioned I might as well keep doing construction and just make the money I was used to making.

On the 4th of July 2000 I figured out what I wanted to do. I have always loved music. I have always loved working with young people. I have always loved preaching the gospel. I was really good with people. Everyone that worked for me were in bands. I had been in bands. I was always giving business advice to them on what contracts to take and not to take. I saw the fields ripe and ready for harvest. I felt that the average person wanted to do the right thing and that if it was convenient for them to do the right thing they would. However, if it were convenient and acceptable to do the wrong thing, they would do that as well. The average music venue or club is a bar that has bands play so that people will come and drink alcohol. What if I had a place that was all about the music? What if I had a place that had a good influence on the youth of the city? What if the music was uplifting and the atmosphere was uplifting?

You see, musicians these days are more powerful than presidents and politicians and preachers. Whatever the bands do, the people follow. If they dye their hair and tattoo their bodies so do the people. If they protest the war, so do the masses. If they do drugs, or drink, or smoke... well you get the point. What if I could do my part to change that? What if I had the opportunity to meet and rub shoulders with the bands that influence the world? If I could let them see some light, maybe they would share that light with the world. Now, I knew this would take time. I knew it would be hard. I knew that I wouldn't get any credit for it. I didn't want to do it for the credit. Someone had to be the guy that shared his faith with Billy Graham. Who was that guy? I don't know. But God does and I'm grateful that he did.

My brother, River and I came up with an idea for a club that would be all ages, all the time. We would have no alcohol or smoking. We would be anti-drug. We would help the youth of America to grow up and be better than we had been. We could have band rehearsal rooms and a recording studio. We would leave room to expand so that we could eventually have a record label for bands that we believed in and possibly other ventures as well. We researched and looked at other clubs. We made some rough sketches of what we needed. I called my realtor and told her my plan. I told everyone I was going to build this club. Almost no one believed me. Most people laughed at me to my face, but some had the decency to do it behind my back. Everyone thought I was crazy.

I started looking at commercial property. I had no idea it was so expensive! I looked at a broken down building in downtown Arlington. All the windows were broken out. Nothing worked. It was condemned. It was like one of the junk houses I was so used to fixing up. I thought I could just write a check and then fix it up and be open within a few months. They wouldn't sell it to me because they wanted someone to buy it that had very "deep pockets". It was a two-story building, but they wanted me to make it into a three-story building. They wanted the bottom floor to be retail, the second floor to be office spaces, and the third floor to be loft apartments. I would have had to do extensive asbestos abatement that would be VERY expensive. And to top it off they wanted $539,000 for it.

The next place was about the same except they wanted $975,000 for it. So, I looked at building the building from the ground up. First of all the city wouldn't let me have the zoning that I needed anywhere I looked. They just didn't want it in their city. I looked at a 3-acre patch of grass. It was $1,500,000. I was ready to give up. I had been looking at leasing a building, but even that would have been about $20,000 a month just for the lease.

Then one day, my realtor (who always works miracles for me) found a building on Division Street that would be perfect. It was a little over an acre of land. It had a parking lot, kind of. It had a building that was 12,500 square feet. The zoning was right. It was under contract to be a porn store. The neighbors protested and the realtor backed out to save her reputation since it was in the papers as a scandal. The owner just wanted to dump it quickly. I looked at it on Saturday, August 26th. I thought about it over the weekend. She wanted $325,000 for it, but she was willing to owner finance $200,000 of it for seven years. On Monday I said yes. We closed on Thursday. It was unbelievable! I had saved up $139,000 and I wrote a check for $125,000 as a down payment. My bank account hadn't been that low in years, but I owned a huge building. I didn't have any time to waste. I started work right away.

11 Living in a Dreamworld

Anyone who has ever owned commercial property and a business can relate to the following long list of disasters. Most businesses fail in the first year. I think it is 85% actually. If I hadn't been so stubborn and unyielding I would have failed also. I could have easily folded at any time and gone bankrupt. No one would have held it against me with all I went through. I am not *that guy* though. Winners never quit and quitters never win. So, I grabbed that bull by the horns and rode it until I broke it. In retrospect, we really just broke each other I suppose.

I had counted the cost of remodeling the building and making it into a club. It was well within my means. It was a stretch, but I could do it. I figured we would just throw some walls up, blow some insulation, put in a stage and some lights, put in a few bathrooms, and bang we would be in business. "Not so" said the building inspectors.

As soon as I bought the property I went to City Hall to get a building permit and to get my electricity turned on. The head building inspector cussed me out. He said that I NEVER should have bought the property without consulting him first. He said even though the zoning on it was right, that there would still be no way that I could meet all the requirements that they would have for me to get a Certificate of Occupancy and actually open my business. He said all this before he even knew what kind of resources I had to work with. This began a long frustrating process of dealing with completely unhelpful inspectors and planners and architects, etc.

I sat in their offices for hours until they would finally see me. I would get small tidbits of information from each one of them and then compile it together into a new plan. Almost every day the plan had to change because of some other code they just found that restricted me from doing what I needed to do. I asked to see their code books. They wouldn't let me check them out and they wouldn't tell me where to get a copy for myself, so I simply sat in the waiting room and looked up codes on my type of building and my type of business. There was a nice lady who worked there. She would come over and give me tips on where to look when no one was watching her. I could tell she was upset about the injustice of the whole thing. She really helped a lot. From time to time they would get tired of looking at me and they would just point me in the right direction.

At long last they gave me an OK to start working on my remodeling project.

I worked on that building day and night until I opened. I worked 20 hours a day, seven days a week, for 10 straight weeks without a break. It cost me everything I had. Because of handicap accessibility and fire codes I had to spend $100,000 more than I had originally intended. I had to mortgage my house, and clean out savings and checking. I racked up $50,000 more in debt on my line of credit, $50,000 more from my home equity, another $80,000 in credit cards. At the end of the whole thing I had spent $545,000! I owed all of my subcontractors. I owed $12,000 on my PA. And I had to borrow money from my family that they didn't have. River talked to my mother behind my back and said "John isn't doing well. It would help if you guys could come up with $20,000 or so and loan it to him for a while." They got $5,000, which I was grateful for.

We finally got a Certificate of Occupancy the day we were supposed to open, December 2nd, 2000. I was bloody and beaten. I was exhausted beyond recognition. I had grown a full beard because I hadn't found time to shave in two and a half months. I was discouraged and disheartened. We built the stage the day before we opened. The Fort Worth Star Telegram came out to do a story on us. They took pictures of us building the stage and put them on the front page of the paper. By this time we were already a political "hot potato". The city people were all in trouble for letting us slip by. I remember my building inspector saying to me "John, I admire your resilience. You jumped through all our hoops and never gave up. Nobody wanted this club to open, but you wouldn't take no for an answer. You might stand bloody, but you do stand." I was touched. He had hit the nail right on the head.

We were moving miter saws and air compressors backstage and trying to make our job site look like a music venue when it happened. The building inspector came at 4:58 on opening day and said "We are going to shut you down." I argued, but they would close in two minutes and we were supposed to open in two hours. I finally negotiated with them and they agreed to reduce our occupant load down from 980 to 600 people until we got the whole thing cleared up. But they assured me that it was only because of the amount of press I had gotten already that they even allowed it. They threatened me and said that the fire marshal WOULD be by to do a headcount that night and they would shut us down with a smile if there was one extra person in there.

It was crushing! The bands had promoted. We had promoted. We had worked hard. Just for them to come and rain on our parade two minutes before closing. I thought it was dirty, but we honored the 600 person occupant load for two months after that until they finally gave us a straight answer. We had to put in three extra fire doors, but we finally got our occupancy.

Opening night was chaos, but it was beautiful chaos. I had spent everything I had. I owed my employees money, lots of it. I didn't even have enough to buy concessions to sell that night. My realtor, Becky, stepped up and bought concessions for me out of her own money. She said it was an honor to know me and that anything she could do to help was her pleasure. People came out of nowhere to help. Until a few hours before, all we had been was a remodeling job that seemed like it would never end. All of the sudden we actually transformed into a music venue. Everyone did their part. About 600 people showed up. We grossed about $10,000 that night.

There were problems and bugs to work out everywhere and it was all my problem, but the crowd never knew the difference. We had to park cars in the grassy field next door to us. It rained heavily that night and lots of cars got stuck in the mud, but I pulled them out with my truck. The night finally ended. We had done it! What had only been a dream before was now a Dreamworld! By the way that is what I called it: Dreamworld Music Complex. We had made the impossible possible. Let me describe it to you. It is 12,500 square feet. That is 50 feet wide and 250 feet long with 19 foot tall ceilings in the main room. The venue had a stage that was 40 feet wide by 30 feet deep by 4 feet tall.

Our main room could hold 980 people. We also had a recording studio and 23 band rehearsal rooms. The bands could practice 24 hours a day, 7 days a week for a monthly fee. If they want they can rent the rooms by the night. Each different aspect of the place created traffic for the others. It was like one stop shopping for a music lover and musician. It got a slow start. We had a lot of bad press. We were on the front page of the papers more than once. We were on the news and the radio. People knew about us, but it wasn't all good. There was another problem. We are all ages so we don't serve alcohol. However, I did let secular bands play at my venue. So, Christian people hated me because I had secular bands, but everyone else hated me because I didn't serve alcohol.

This was a constant struggle. We continued to have problems from the city. They would send out everyone they had. I got visits from the TABC, The Health Department, The Fire Marshal, The Police, Code Enforcement, and so on. We had undercover cops and the FBI out on more than one occasion. They threatened our neighbor and forbid him to let us use the grassy parking lot for overflow parking. They would tow cars when we had big shows. I lost more business than I can ever even know. It was very disheartening. The city was determined to get rid of me.

I was barely scraping by. I was upside-down on everything. All I was paying was interest and lots of it. I owed everybody lots of money. I couldn't get a breath. I never had enough, but I also never gave up. We tried lots of different things. We rented the building out to a friend of mine to start a church on Sunday mornings. We tried every type of music to see which ones brought people out. We tried doing a rave on New Year's Eve of 2000. I lost money. Only 14 people showed up. Later someone offered us $500 to have another rave. I took the money. The promoter lost money. Only a handful of people showed up.

The promoter that had lost money told someone that we would host raves. One of our rival clubs was told that they couldn't have raves anymore on the day of a big show. They needed a new venue and we were it. We already had a show that night, but they were willing to pay me $2,500 to rent the venue after our other concert that night. I thought it was dumb of them, but I needed the money so I said yes.

I had never met my real father and Lana had been looking for him for a few years. He had been homeless for about 30 years or so. He had no driver's license or home address. There was no getting in touch with him, but she had written a letter to a friend of his about a year earlier. He showed up on February 17th, 2001. I had never even seen a picture of my father, Sky, until about a year earlier. I went to go pick him up when he called me. He had very long hair and a very long beard, both down to his waist. He carried everything he owned on his back. He was intelligent, but delusional.

I bought him something to eat and took him back to the club. He said that I could say he was someone that was working for me so that he wouldn't embarrass me. I told him that if anyone asked I would tell the truth, that he was my father. I have never been ashamed of the truth. If someone doesn't like it then they can deal with it, but I won't lie and cover up the truth. We talked for a while. He got me alone behind the building and started to freak out. He started talking to people that weren't there and grabbing things that weren't there.

He started saying some mumbo-jumbo that didn't make any sense. He said, " I have saved the world several times over, but the world doesn't want to be saved. It keeps going back to its sin. Jesus hates you. He wants to eat your soul spark. He wants to feed on you. The devil is his brother and he hates you too. They want me dead for telling their secrets. I have to be careful. They listen to everything. They look on the Internet and tap the phone lines, but they also use psychic powers to read our minds. So, I have to train myself to not think about things for too long or they will find me and kill me. They want me dead. I can save you right now. Bang! There is life! Do you want it? Bang! There is death and hell! Is that what you choose?"

He was waving his hands around and pointing in the air. He would go into trances and then mumble nonsense. It was very disturbing. He looked troubled. I wish I could do justice to his insanity. It just sounds so normal when I say it in comparison. I thought for a moment and I said, " You don't have to worry about that when you are with me. River and I have set up psychic blockers and debugged all of our phones and Internet. When you are in our homes, our cars, or Dreamworld then you are safe from all that." He took a deep breath and he let out a sigh of relief. He simply looked at me calmly and said "Thank you! That was so thoughtful of you."

I almost laughed out loud, but then I realized he was serious so I just went with it. If it calmed him down from that delirious fit then I was happy. River showed up later and he tried the same thing with him. River wasn't having it. He nipped it in the bud. He said, "I don't care about any of that stuff. Tell me about you. I want to know about your life and then I'll tell you about mine. That's it." He calmed down again.

He told River about how he had been all over the world. He told a story about when he was on a small boat somewhere in the Pacific Ocean. He was sleeping and one of the people on the boat stole his guitar from him. He asked a few people about it, but no one was talking. He shamelessly walked to the biggest group of people on the boat and simply said " I am an angel of God. You have stolen my harp. If you don't give back my guitar I will call down all the wrath of God on this boat and you will all be sorry." Apparently it was very convincing because the guitar instantly appeared and they all treated him like a deity for the rest of the trip.

He told another story about how some cowboys had seen him walking down the highway one night and they all proceeded to beat him bloody and leave him in a ditch to die. What is the point of beating up a homeless man that is doing no harm to anyone? It is a sad account of our world in my opinion.

He pulled out this guitar that was mostly duct tape and started trying to tune it in some weird way. By this time I had given up all hope. I'm sure I rolled my eyes. Then he pulled out this flute that he had made for me some twenty years earlier and had been carrying around for all that time. He started rubbing it back and forth on the twelfth fret like a harmonic. He said, "it takes a minute, but when it happens it sounds like angels singing. I discovered it. I call it a triple harmonic." An annoying noise came out and I got ready to suffer through some more insanity. Then, it happened and he was right, it did sound like angels singing. I had never heard anything like it before. It was beautiful! Then he started playing songs in this weird tuning, and he started singing. It was amazing! It was like the only time he could get himself in tune was when he was playing and singing music. Everything else just took a backseat. He is very talented. He has written thousands of songs. He has made copies of several hundred of them for us. I asked him to teach me the tuning, which he did.

Him and River and myself jammed together for a few hours. It was very freeing. The whole thing touched me. He knew lots of things about massages and health food. He gave me a massage and said something like "this part of your back is tense, that means blah, blah, blah." I forget what it was now, but he was right! He knew a lot more than he let on. He had been everywhere and although his mind was a mess from too much acid, he deserved my respect. He had seen a lot more than I could ever hope to see. He had wisdom from years of fearless exploration. Had he lost his mind somewhere along the way? Yes. But that didn't change the fact that he still had things that I could learn from him.

He stayed up at the club with us that night. We had our concert and then the parking lot started to fill up for the rave that would happen after the concert. We were paid the $2,500 as if it were nothing. I left the promoter in charge for a minute while I went to my office. When I came back there were wall-to-wall people. It took me ten minutes to get from one end of the club to the other end because of the crowd. There were at least 1,500 people in the club that had each paid $25 to see this show! I thought I was just going to take this guy's money, but he was for real!

Then the drugs started. There was ecstasy everywhere. People were lighting joints in the building. There were dog piles of people groping each other. Girls were getting naked. People were throwing up. It was out of control. Someone came over from the parking lot and said that an old guy named Norman had just come up and said, " I am going to shut this place down. I have never liked it anyway. I am calling the police and the fire marshal and the mayor. I used to be the head of human resources and I will shut this place down if it is the last thing I do."

I didn't think anything of it. I was far too busy kicking people out for doing drugs. It was a steady string. We would kick a group out and then another one would be doing the same thing. Then the cops showed up and started blaming me for the whole thing. They raided the place. Police were walking me around saying "look there are kids puking and doing drugs. Do you know what this Vick's is for? Ecstasy! Everyone has pacifiers to keep their teeth from chattering while they are doing X. It smells like pot in here. Those kids are drunk. What kind of a place are you running here?" They threatened to shut me down for good.

I told them that I didn't think anyone would show up for this thing. I told them about the raves we had had earlier and what a flop they were. The promoter had disappeared with about $38,000. He had several pieces of luggage full of money. The whole thing fell on me. It was the beginning of the end for me, but I didn't know it yet. Then the Fire Marshal showed up because we were over occupied. He didn't seem to care at all. He seemed irritated that the police had woken him up at 2 am for such a petty thing as this. He said that the country bar on the other side of town over occupied all the time and they just told them to not let anyone else in for the rest of the night. I agreed and thanked him for his time. The cops were at my place for the rest of the night.

They didn't arrest me for anything or write me a ticket because I was cooperating and it really wasn't my fault. I was also doing everything in my power to make it right. Eventually they wrote me a ticket for "unreasonable noise". I was zoned in a light industrial zone. The closest business that was open at that time was at least 10 miles away. The cops told me to take the ticket and thank them for not arresting me. I was going to pay the ticket, but then someone tipped me off that the city was trying to build a grievance against me so they could shut me down. So, I found a lawyer who would defend me for $300. He said it was refreshing to defend someone who was actually innocent. Later, I referred him to someone I knew that had gotten in some trouble. I asked if he would take a case like that. He said, "You mean defend criminals? John, that's what I do. I am a defense lawyer."

As the weeks went by, the police came more and more. I ended up knowing them all by name. I assured them that I had remedied the problem. I tried to work with them in every way possible. They made it seem as if the noise complaints were the main issue. I had meetings with experts and police. I invited the man that was calling in the noise complaints to come and see the place. It was the same guy that had threatened to shut me down. He called every night, even if we weren't open. He called the police over 300 times a month. It was very frustrating.

He was afraid we would lower his property value. He was unyielding. He called the police and the mayor every night for years. He was a thorn in my side. I built 3-foot thick walls full of sand, insulation, and several layers of well-designed walls to try to keep the noise from reaching his house that was over a mile away until I finally realized it was not about the noise. It was never about the noise. It was about people that looked different and a crowd he was afraid of.

Norman was my worst nightmare and my best friend all at the same time. He cost me hundreds of thousands of dollars and lots of sleepless nights, but he overdid it so much that the police got tired of hearing him complain, so they finally lost interest. And even though he had a lot of power in the city from his previous position no one liked him. He had always been mean to everyone, so when the time came no one wanted to help him out.

I'll tell more about the noise complaints later. There were other things going on at the same time. One week after the police raided me, my wife called me during a concert. I had been busy working and dealing with all the problems that the club had given me and I knew I had neglected her recently. She said she was having a panic attack and that she needed to go to the hospital. I tried to talk her through it. She made me feel like dirt because I didn't drop everything and take her to the emergency room. She came up to the club to let me know what a jerk I was. I did feel pretty bad.

She left and then River's wife gave me a note. It was February 25th, 2001, a day that will echo through the halls of my memory for the rest of my life. I knew I worked too much and I knew we were having some problems because of our financial situation at the moment so I thought this would be another one of those "you need to spend more time with me and the kids" notes. Nope. I was blind-sided. Lana always said that if I ever cheated on her that she would divorce me without a thought. She would say all kinds of graphic things about what she would do to me if I ever did cheat on her. I never wanted to cheat on her. Honestly, I never thought she would cheat on me either. I met her in church. She was a good mother. Not always the best wife, but I loved her.

The note went something like this:

"Dear John,

I love you and I will always love you. You have been working a lot lately. I have been crying out for attention, but you are too busy to notice. I met some friends and we have been hanging out a lot lately. They brought out some marijuana and started smoking it. You know that I have always wanted to try it and I didn't think it would hurt anything, so I did. At first I didn't feel anything, but then everything got fuzzy. This guy put on a condom and started having sex with me. I thought it was you. Then I realized it wasn't and I told him to get off of me. I grabbed my purse and left. I threw up. I wish I could take it back.

I don't want to be friends with them anymore. I don't want to be a hippy any more. I want to be your wife. I love you. You were right about drugs. Please take me back and we can have a wonderful life together.

Your wife forever,

Lana"

That is a paraphrase, but it is close. The real note was a lot longer and she beat around the bush more. I threw away the real note a long time ago. Needless to say I was devastated and heartbroken. They say the phases of grief are: shock, denial, anger, depression, and acceptance, and hopefully forgiveness. I think it is safe to say I was shocked at first. I didn't see it coming at all. We argued sometimes, but it was still a lot less than most couples I knew. I just didn't understand why she would do something like that to me. It didn't make any sense. I gave her everything she wanted and everything she needed. Anything she asked for I gave her without question. I trusted her with everything. I was married for life and I never held anything back. The way the note was written implied that this guy had raped her. It also said how sorry she was and although I was upset I wanted to make the whole thing work.

I felt sorry for her more than anything. It must be a terrible feeling to be able to do that to your spouse. I guess you never really know the way you will react in a situation until you are put in it. I just wanted to make it right. I thought "What kind of a man would I be to ask forgiveness from God from all the things I had done and not forgive my own wife for what she had done to me?"

I naturally had a lot of questions running through my mind. I knew she hadn't told me the whole truth. I had been high plenty of times and nothing like that ever happened. I also knew that it took a lot of time for a guy to get her undressed and himself undressed, get "ready", put on a condom, and start having sex with her. There was plenty of time to realize it wasn't me. Marijuana doesn't get you that far out of it. She knew it wasn't me...and that hurt.

I asked River and his wife what they knew about the whole situation. They played dumb and gave me a few clues, but I figured that they knew more than they were letting on. I wanted to know who this guy was that had slept with my wife. Was it someone I knew? He had to be some kind of rich stud to take her away from me. After all, I wasn't bad looking. I was strong and able. I made sure she was satisfied every time. And although times were hard I still made better money than anyone I knew. So who was this guy? I had to know. There would be no way that I would let him smugly get away with this. I didn't want to have him come into my house and shake my hand and eat my food and sit on my furniture and have him be smiling inside all the while knowing that he had screwed my wife. That wasn't going to happen. I had to know.

I didn't know what the right thing to do was. I hadn't planned for this at all. How do you deal with something like this in a righteous way? I resolved to try to forgive her and make it work somehow. The concert finally ended and I went home. The kids were asleep, Lana wasn't. She tried to act like it was nothing and that it would all be all right if we just didn't talk about it. I cried a lot. She lied a lot. I finally got it out of her that it was a guy that worked at a health food store that she went to. His name was Brad. The way she talked about him you would think he was a saint. I told her I would forgive her and take her back... if she **never** saw him again at all. She couldn't go to that store anymore. I didn't want her calling him or answering his calls. I didn't want her at his house and I definitely didn't want him at my house. If she went back to him then she would lose me forever and that was the only way I would take her back.

She groveled a lot and said how sorry she was and how bad she wanted it to work between us. I believed her and I took her back. I let it go and didn't tell anyone. I covered for her to save her from the humiliation that she would face if anyone knew. River and his wife knew and Joel and his wife knew (Joel was a guy that worked for me and he was there when I got the note) but no one else knew. So I kept my mouth shut about it and I didn't even bring it up to her. I told her I would forgive her and not bring it up, so I did.

Inside I was hurting though. I felt so betrayed. I felt like a failure. I felt inadequate. It felt like a huge dumpster had been lowered on my chest. It was hard to breathe. It was hard to focus on work or anything else for that matter. It was always on my mind. The thought of your wife with someone else is a haunting thought that doesn't quickly heal.

That night she had also come clean on a lot of other things. She had been smoking for the last year behind my back and I didn't know about it, but everyone else did. That was very unsettling. How can your spouse smoke for a year without you knowing it? How can she keep covering up a lie for that long and me not even suspect? She had gotten high several times, not just once. In fact, I got the feeling that she was a regular user. The more I paid attention the more I realized that she only hung out with people that were probably druggies. I had never really paid attention because I did too at the club, but that was my business and I didn't do what they did.

I also knew she had been drinking a lot recently. I thought she would get sick of it after a while, but she was drinking quite a bit. I caught her in several lies, things that she didn't have to lie about. She would take money out of my wallet while I was sleeping and then lie about it. If she wanted money all she had to do was ask. So why lie? When I asked her about it all she had to say was "Yes, I needed money for_____". That would have been the end of it.

One night she called me while I was having a concert. She was having another panic attack. She had been having a lot of those recently. She skated around the actual issue for a while, but she finally told me what was bothering her. She was afraid that she might be pregnant or have a venereal disease. She had always been a hypochondriac, but I didn't think she was that naive. If he wore a condom and stopped before he finished then it was pretty much impossible.... unless she had been lying.

I got it out of her that they had been together several times, not just once. She had given him oral sex on more than one occasion. Some of these times had been since she confessed to me. All of the sudden this wasn't one slip up, and it wasn't anything like the way she had described it to me. This was a full-blown affair. I was furious! She had already gone to some clinic to get tested, but the results hadn't come back yet.

I told River about what she had said. He didn't seem the least bit surprised. He told me that the only reason Lana had told me about the affair was because he found out about it through his wife. Joel's wife and River's wife had found out a while back, but they told her to never tell me at all. River's wife has a big mouth and so it got back to River. River told Lana "You are dirty for doing that to John. He is a good man and he is my brother. You will tell him what you did or else I will! I have never liked you anyway and my story will be a lot worse than yours." So the only reason she told me at all was not that she felt bad for cheating, but because she felt bad for being caught!

178

Someone came out to my club and said "I see your wife all the time up at _____" (the health food store where she wasn't supposed to be). I asked when the last time he saw her there was and he said, "I talked to her and the kids yesterday. Actually, several people came to me saying things like that. I had let it go for a while and I was willing to forgive her for things done in the past, but this had to stop. She was still lying to me and cheating. I decided to meet this Brad guy. I went up to the store where he worked and asked for him. They unknowingly gave me a description of him, but he wasn't there at the time.

I came back later and saw him working. He didn't know me, so I just watched him for a while. He was tall and fat. He probably weighed over 250 pounds. He was unkempt and dirty. Dirty like he didn't take showers, dirty. He had pork chop side burns and thick horn rimmed glasses. He had a high-pitched, whiny voice. He worked in the meat department and didn't look like he was in charge. He made $8 an hour and I knew he lived in an apartment with roommates. I was almost disappointed. How humiliating! If she had cheated with a good looking, young, fit doctor I could almost understand. But this guy! She preferred this idiot over me? It didn't make sense.

After a while he noticed me looking at him and asked if he could help me. I asked if he knew Lana and he said yes. I asked if he was screwing her. He got a little nervous and then hesitantly said yes. Then he asked why. I got a little closer to him and I said, "Because she is my wife." Well, he wasn't just a fat nerd. He was a coward too. Which was no surprise. He got really scared and started apologizing and making excuses. He said, " Man, I am so sorry. I never wanted anything to happen, but she kept pushing it. We went out a few times and she would complain about you then she started holding my hand. She told me she loved me. It really freaked me out. She won't leave me alone! I don't know what to do. We did sleep together. I just want her to leave me alone."

Now I knew he probably would have said anything to get away from me at that moment. I was stronger than him and madder than him. I knew that some of what he was saying was a lie, but I also knew that some of what he was saying was true. That made me even madder at Lana. She had pursued him! Was I really that bad that she had to replace me with this loser?

I told him to never talk to my wife again. I said, " I don't care if she strips down naked in front of you and offers you anything you want. I don't care if it is all her fault. If I find out you have so much as talked to her again you will regret it." I'll admit it was an idle threat. I wouldn't have hurt anyone anyway. But it scared him. He kept groveling like a coward as I walked away.

I didn't tell Lana what I did because I wanted to see how long it was until they saw each other again and then I would know that she knew. Needless to say it didn't take long. They were seeing each other all the time. I'll get back to this story in a minute. I have to tell you what else was going on at the same time. My life was under fire on every side. I might have been able to handle any one of these things, but I was being overrun with tragedy.

12   Trial By Fire

In the meantime, I was facing the very serious threat of bankruptcy and having my club shut down by the city. I found out that the unreasonable noise ticket that I got on February 18th could be up to $2,100! The police came by several times a week to harass me. It seems that our good friend Norman had rallied some neighbors to help call the police every night. But he wouldn't let that stop him; he made time in his busy schedule every night to call the police himself as well. The cops would come by on nights when we were closed and say they were there for noise complaints. They would come by on nights that were all acoustic... for noise complaints. They even came by one night when we had a power failure for a noise complaint.

Some of the cops started catching on that it was getting ridiculous, but they were under orders from above. If a cop started becoming too friendly to us they were transferred. I know that sounds paranoid, but that is the way it happened. I had to find a way to defend myself form this injustice, so I looked into the law...extensively. I posted copies of the law all over my club: in my office, by the sound booth and monitor board, by the front door, by the back door, backstage, and by the concession stand. The law on unreasonable noise says that:

"A noise is presumed to be unreasonable if the noise exceeds decibel levels of 85 after the person making the noise receives notice from a magistrate or peace officer that the noise is a public nuisance."

To put that in perspective a starter's pistol is 150 decibels, a chainsaw is 120 decibels, a leaf blower is 110 decibels, a lawn mower is 95 decibels, a baby crying is 110 decibels. These are all measured right next to the source. However, in this case the noise has to be 85 decibels at the point of complaint. In other words it has to be 85 decibels a mile away at the guy's house that is complaining. The first ticket we got the cops acted like I was an idiot to own a music venue and not own a decibel reader, so I bought one. We did tests.

Here is what we found. With the doors of the club open, standing ten feet away from the building, our PA only put out 85 decibels when it was so loud that you couldn't stand it. At our normal volume it was only 65 decibels ten feet away from the building. So, then we walked to the back of the property, and the property behind ours. By the time you got that far you couldn't hear anything at all. It wouldn't even register on the decibel reader at all. Nothing! So then we got in a car and drove a mile and a half to Norman's house. Since we couldn't hear anything we called and had the PA turned up. We never heard anything. Just as I suspected it was never about sound at all. It was about prejudice. We brought freaky looking people to our place and it scared the powers that be.

The next time the cops came out I told them about our experiment and I asked if they would walk to the back of the property and drive to the neighborhood that was complaining. The cop was resistant at first, but finally agreed. He left two other cops with River to make sure that we didn't play with the volume while he was gone. He only did that because I insisted that he leave someone to make sure we weren't being deceitful with him. We walked to the back of the property and he said, "You are right you can't hear anything, but let's go to the neighborhood." I agreed.

We drove in his car to the neighborhood. It was funny to watch him squirm. First we went to Norman's house and parked the car. No noise. Then he rolled down the windows. Still no noise, then he turned the car off. Nothing. Then we got out of the car and walked closer to the club. Nothing. Then we got back in the car and drove somewhere else and did the same thing. After the third stop he said, "Do you hear that?" I said "no, unless you mean the airplane." We waited for the airplane, and then some cars to pass, then a train went by, then the crickets were chirping.

Finally there was a lull in absolutely everything and he said, "Now, do you hear it?" I said "I suppose if it will make you happy, but no, not really. The guy lives under one of the busiest airports in the world. At any given time there are 14 planes within eyesight. He lives right off a road that has 150,000 cars a day drive on it. He lives 200 feet away from railroad tracks that have 4 trains an hour barreling through. There are birds and lawn mowers and crickets and background noise everywhere. And you want me to believe that even though you can't hear my music at all that I am a public nuisance for unreasonable noise?"

He looked at me and said "You know what, you are right. This is petty. This is just rich people with too much time on their hands. He had the other cops write down the decibel reading at the time we did the test. He said to me "if you keep the music at this level you won't get any more tickets. You have my word." Finally we had won!

Just kidding. That same cop wrote me another ticket less than a week later. He refused to look at our decibel reader or go to the neighborhood. When I asked him about giving his word, he denied ever saying such a ridiculous thing and wrote the ticket anyway. I think he felt bad about writing the ticket and so he backed off a little. As soon as that happened he got transferred and a new cop became the sergeant on our beat. His name was Justin.

After the inconsistencies I had been dealing with I decided to start recording my conversations with Arlington's finest. I bought one of those tiny recorders. We already had video cameras set up all over the place that recorded everything that happened at the club. I was tired of being abused and lied to. I was going to fight back. I had had enough. I knew I didn't have the resources that they did so I had to be creative. I wrote a five page story about how Dreamworld had started, what my intentions were with the place, and what the cops and the city had done to persecute me. It was called "Does This Seem Right To You?" At the bottom of the article I put the mayor's e-mail address.

Honestly, I just hoped that someone up high would get on my website and read it and realize that we weren't what they thought. I hoped that they would just leave us alone. They all read it, but so did everyone else. Every club around put links from their website to that page on mine. Apparently, this is the way that cities treat all clubs. I wasn't the only one.

Usually they scare them away a lot quicker. A lot of people have addictions or habits or warrants or something that they can threaten with. I didn't. I am clean. I don't do drugs. I don't drink alcohol. I don't use tobacco. I don't cuss. I don't go to strip clubs. I am faithful to my wife. There is no scandal to threaten me with, so they were powerless. Then to top it off I was pleading "not guilty" to the noise complaints and I told the prosecutor that I wanted a jury trial since I didn't think I would get a fair trial from a judge. Since I hadn't been convicted of any of the noise complaints and I didn't pay them (which would be pleading guilty) then they couldn't build a grievance against me or my club.

I told the prosecutor when she tried to plea bargain with me that "if and when this goes to court I will call every newspaper, radio station, TV news channel, magazine, etc. and personally invite them to witness the trial. So, by all means, please give me a trial as soon as possible." She shrugged and said, "Do whatever you want."

My little website article was getting a lot of attention. It was getting about 200 hits a day. Letters and e-mails were pouring in to the mayor's office from all over the country. I had famous bands that had played at my club writing e-mails. Parents and kids, young adults, friends, other business owners, everyone was writing. Everywhere I went someone would say, "I read that thing you wrote. I can't believe they are doing that to you. We are with you, man. You can beat them!" It was great.

I got interviewed for another newspaper article and when I asked what the reporter's angle was on this story he told me that it was because of the big city council meeting tonight. I had no idea they were having a city council meeting about me. Personally, I think you should tell someone when he is the topic of discussion at a government meeting, but apparently that isn't the case. Nevertheless, I got all my people together and we went to the meeting that night unannounced. The roster for the evening said:

1) Public transportation in Arlington
2) Noise complaints at Dreamworld

It didn't say noise complaints in general or at nightclubs or any other vague statement. It said noise complaints at Dreamworld! I wasn't notified. As you have probably already noticed I remember the cops that come out to my place. I learn their names. I pay attention. Some cop got on the stand that I had never seen before and testified that the manager of Dreamworld was completely unwilling to cooperate with the city and that he recommended that it be shut down. He proceeded to say that there were repeated cases of drugs and underage drinking at Dreamworld and that the place was a nuisance to the city. I sat and listened for a while and then from the crowd I said, "That is a lie!"

The whole crowd was shocked. They all turned and looked at me. A lot of people started whispering. Someone came up and whispered in the mayor's ear. He stopped the whole meeting and said "It is my understanding that the manager of Dreamworld might possibly be in the room with us tonight." I raised my hand and said, "I'm right here." He pretended not to see me and asked if anyone knew whether or not I might be in the room. I repeated myself several times before he acknowledged me.

He asked me to take the stand and swore me in. I started to tell of the injustice of the whole situation and then said how much I had already done to try to remedy the situation. That I had built more walls and put up more insulation. That I had meetings with the neighbors, the police, and the press. I started to tell him what else was going on and he simply said, "I've heard enough. You can sit down now. Thank you." I didn't ever get to finish defending myself, but I had stopped the mock trial that was going on.

Several weeks went by and I tried to have a meeting with the mayor and the chief of police and the city manager. They were all too busy to see me. It was amazing that I was the top priority in the town as far as the police were concerned and a big enough deal to have a city council meeting about, but they couldn't find time to even return my phone calls. And when I went in person and waited for hours they still couldn't see me. I e-mailed my city council member to try to defend myself.

He said the city didn't have anything against me or my club and welcomed me to come and present my case before the city council that night. I told him that I would love to, but it was my son's birthday that night and I had to be at his party at 6:30. Then I invited him to come to a show that Friday night to see for himself that Dreamworld was not what it had been portrayed as. Later that night I got a phone call on my cell phone. It was Dennis, my monitor guy. He said there were cops everywhere and that the alarm was going off.

I rushed up to the club. I passed a cop car on the way there that was leaving my club. When I got there the alarms were going off and the backstage door was wide open. I wondered why my alarm company hadn't called me yet. I went through the building, but no one was there and nothing seemed to be missing. I called my alarm company to see what had happened. They said that they hadn't received a signal and as far as they were concerned nothing had happened. They had never called me or the police. If the cops had been there it wasn't because they had called. I was standing in front of my building on the phone and I saw a cop car driving by so I started waving him down. He saw me and put on his breaks. Then he recognized me and turned the other way. He pretended not to see me. He sped up and drove away.

A few minutes later another cop did the same thing. I was confused. I talked to Dennis and he told me what time the whole thing happened. By this time there was a big group of people all trying to figure out what in the world just happened. We reviewed the videotapes and this is what we found. A cop, who will remain nameless even though I know his name, walked into the front doors. He tried to open both the hallway doors, but they require a code so he couldn't get in. He walked around to the backstage door and a few minutes later came into the backstage area. The alarm started to sound. We could see the sirens going off up front. He had to hear the sirens, but he didn't even flinch. He went out of sight for a few minutes and then started to walk out. Then he stopped, reached in his pocket, turned around, and threw something down on the table.

He then left and went to the front doors again. By that time Dennis was there and the cop asked to get inside the office so he could use the phone. A girl who was there at the time offered to let him use her cell phone, but he said it had to be a landline. He insisted on being let inside. Dennis didn't have a key so the cop left.

We wanted to see what he put on the table backstage, so we went back there. On the table was a baggie full of white powder. One of the guys opened it, stuck his finger in and licked it, and said, "It is cocaine!" A thousand questions ran through my head. Where else had they planted drugs? Dreamworld was huge and there were nooks and crannies everywhere to hide stuff in. They could have thrown a bag of drugs anywhere back in the venue! Then we heard a helicopter circling above us. We heard sirens coming our way. I called Lana and said, "They have planted drugs in the building. They are coming right now. I'm sure they will arrest me. Whatever happens you have to know I am innocent. I am telling you know before it happens. They are framing me." She got very scared, and to be honest so did I.

I thought for a moment and then I called the cops. They didn't know I had cameras. They were hidden and small. I called on my cell phone, which wasn't listed as a Dreamworld number. The conversation went like this:

"911 emergency"

"This is John Tunnell from..."

"Yes, we know who you are. From Dreamworld, right?"

"At 3102 West..."

"Yes, we know where you are."

"My burglar alarm is going off and someone has broken into my building..."

"Where did they break in, that backstage door?"

"Yes, how did you know that? Anyway, can I talk to someone in charge?"

I got the sergeant in charge on the phone and he seemed very disinterested in helping me, but he knew all kinds of intimate details about the situation. Finally, I said, "One of your cops broke in my building and planted drugs." He was very skeptical, but a little cautious. He wasn't going to do anything about it **until** I said "I have the whole thing on video tape. Do you want to see it before the press does?" At which point he got scared. He said "You have it on tape?" I reaffirmed that I did in fact have it on tape and he said, "I'll be right there!" In less than three minutes he was at my front door. I showed him the tape several times. It was painfully obvious what had happened. He thought for a moment and said, "There were some phone lines down in your area. I'm sure the officer was just making sure you were alright."

I disagreed with him and asked to file a report and make a record of the whole thing. He refused to make a report and dismissed the whole thing as inconclusive. After he left, I made copies of the tape and put one in my safe and others in safe places. I thought it was very coincidental that I had told my city council person earlier that day that I had to be at my son's birthday party at 6:30 and that the cop had showed up at 6:47 to break in the building. I also thought it was suspicious that my alarm wires had been cut and that they were just out of view of the camera in the exact direction of where the cop had disappeared from view for a few minutes. I also thought it was quite a coincidence that all the cops and even the 911 operator knew so much about the crime before they had been told anything.

That Friday we had a show that should have been really good, but was a total flop. Half way through the show I went up to the gas station to get something only to find that the road had been blocked off on both sides of my club so that no one could come or go. I asked one of the cops what was going on and they said that there was a huge gas leak and they had to shut down the road while they fixed the leak. Several things about that struck me as odd.

1) It happened on the night I told my city council man that we were having a big show that he should come and see.

2) Although they redirected traffic and had at least 10 cops and several fire trucks and lots of machinery and personnel no one came to tell me that there was a gas leak just two doors down from me. I had a crowd of people inside that all could have died from an explosion, but no one told me that my patrons were at risk. However, three days earlier a cop was so concerned about our phone lines that he broke in the building to make sure we were all right.

3) I didn't smell any gas. I know enough about gas leaks to know what it smells like.

You can call me paranoid if you like, but there were an awful lot of coincidences that just didn't seem right to me. Of course no one would file a report and I couldn't prove it, and the press didn't want to lose the leads to a lot of other "juicy stories".

About a week later I was leaving Dreamworld at about 3 am. This car was driving next to me and I didn't think much of it. I sped up a little and then the car next to me sped up as well. I slowed down and so did the other car. It wouldn't get off of me and the driver seemed to be trying to get my attention. So, I turned and looked at the car. There was a girl dressed like a hooker and she was trying to get me to pull over. She was making gestures and so I just sped up my truck and kept going. She wouldn't give up, though. She just kept trying to get me to pull over.

I was in the right lane and she was in the left lane. The light in front of us turned yellow and so I sped up as if I was going to run the light. She also sped up. At the last second I made a right turn at the light instead of running it. She ran the light and I was relieved... for a moment. She stopped in the middle of the road, backed up, and started to follow me again. I noticed that she was driving a flashy sports car and that there was a sedan driving behind her the whole time. It wasn't as obvious until she backed up and followed me at the turn, and so did the sedan!

By now we were almost at my house. I was starting to think "How am I going to explain this to my wife? I don't want this girl knowing where I live!" I decided to just keep driving past my house and drive around until I shook her. As I'm thinking this I notice that she has pulled up next to me even though we are driving on a one lane road! I stopped at the red light and tried to ignore the fact that this girl was on the wrong side of the road next to me.

She was honking and waving her arms around and so finally I just looked at her. She made an "O" shape with her hand, opened her mouth, and moved her hand back and forth in front of it. She asked if I wanted a oral sex. I was more than a little shocked. I shook my head "no" and looked the other way. Just when I thought I would have her chasing me for the rest of the night, she pulled in front of me and drove away. The other car followed her.

In some places that may be normal, but not where I live. That is the only time that has ever happened to me. I drove home and told Lana about it as soon as I got there. She was asleep and didn't seem to care that much. It seemed to me that the whole thing was a set-up, a sting to try to get me to fall. The cops had already tried every way they could to put me out of business. I think they figured that any guy given that opportunity would fall for it and so they could say that an "All Ages night club owner was caught soliciting a prostitute." Maybe I'm wrong. Who knows? I know that stuff like that happens all the time. I know people abuse their power for personal agendas all the time. And it was common knowledge that the police didn't like me.

The sad thing is that when we opened Dreamworld we tried so hard to work with the city and all its authorities to make Arlington a better place. None of them would even talk to me. They had their prejudices about me before I ever began and they were determined to watch me fall, even if they had to push me a little so I would fall. I can't tell you how incredibly disheartening it is to never measure up or be given a fair chance. Prejudice is the same whether it is about skin color or hair color or personal preference.

It is judging someone before you get to know them. Most people do that to some degree. You almost have to. But prejudice reeks of ignorance. The real display of ignorance comes when the person being judged exceeds your expectations, but you simply come up with a new judgment or excuse as to why you should still hate them. It is when the victim can do no right in the eyes of his persecutor, no matter how hard he tries. People really should learn that in the long run everyone is hurt by this mentality. Obviously, the people being hated are hurt, but so is the ignorant "good old boy" that seeks to inflict so much pain.

You see after long enough a person starts to break inside and eventually they snap. If you want a man to act like a decent man, then treat him like a decent man. Even a criminal will eventually turn around if he feels like someone truly believes in him. And even a good citizen will start to act like a criminal if you treat him like one for long enough. There comes a point where you realize that the people you are trying to please are simply unpleasable. You realize that all the hoops you jump through are only precursors to more hoops for you to jump through. Shortly after this hopelessness sets in, then frustration and anger take hold of you and then bad things start to happen.

There should be justice in the justice system, but it is rare. There should be human decency and compassion, but it is rare as well. We should look more at the intent of the law, than the letter of the law. Common sense should enter into the equation at some point. The media should care more about truth then about money.

Everyone should get a fair chance. If they work hard and invest their life savings into something they should be given a little grace, shouldn't they? Shouldn't they at least be given a shot? God help the man that just wants to do the right thing and has to do it all himself.

I didn't have it in me to be a criminal any more. I mean I know I could have done it. I just didn't want to fall. So, instead of lashing back out at the world my heart just kind of died inside. It is hard to explain to someone who hasn't experienced it. I felt like I was running endlessly and there was no finish line and no reward. I felt like there was really no hope. My head knew there was hope, but I didn't FEEL it. I felt like... I wanted to die.

Then to add insult to injury I came home to an empty house and another letter from Lana. She said she was sick of pretending. Everything was gone. So was my family. She kicked me when I was down. She left me right when I needed her the most. It is so cowardly to leave a note to end a marriage. Talk to me face to face. At least give me that. I gave her everything I had, our children, and ten years of my life and she couldn't even tell me how bad she hated me to my face? I felt crushed. Truly crushed. I had never prepared for our marriage to end.

When I said, "till death do us part," I meant it. I never held anything back. I never had a back-up plan. I never looked at other girls. I never cheated on her or even thought about it. I never beat her. I had tried so hard to be a good man. I made it a point to be a good father and a good husband. I did what I said I would do in every area of my life. I was a man of my word. And in return, I got this. Words cannot explain the despair that I felt at that moment.

I talked her into coming back home after a few days. She said she would change and I agreed to make adjustments for her as well. But it was never the same. The first time I took her back was humiliating and a huge step for me, but now it was just becoming routine. Needless to say she kept leaving me. Every few weeks I would come home to an empty house and an empty bank account. I finally opened a second bank account that she didn't know about and only kept enough in our mutual bank account to pay the bills and be believable.

I remember Lana's birthday in 2001. You probably do too, actually. It was September 11th. The World Trade Center fell that morning and our country fell apart. It was a huge blow to the world and we have never really been the same since. We are still dealing with issues from 9/11. Everyone thought the world would end because of that, but it didn't. We have to pick up the pieces and move on. We have to rebuild. The economy took a huge hit and no one wanted to spend any money. No one wanted to be in a crowded area either, like a music venue for example. I think you see where this is going.

Business went from bad to worse on September 11th, 2001. I know it is selfish to think like that, but my life was pretty bad at the time and I was having a hard time keeping my head above water. The whole thing was overwhelming. We had a bunch of national and international bands that cancelled on us because they were afraid of flying. The most notable was a metal tour that was coming from Europe. It was a lot of big name death metal and black metal bands. They sing about death and destruction all the time, but they were too afraid to get on an airplane to come to America. I lost money or barely broke even on every national show since 9/11. I used to make lots of money on national shows, not anymore.

So, two days after Lana's birthday she tells me that she is going to this Renaissance Festival in Houston. I was a little shocked. She hadn't said anything about it and then all of the sudden she was just going that day. She said she would just be there for the weekend, but she packed a lot of stuff. Friday night she called our home phone number when she knew I would be having a concert and said she was staying for another week or so because they had offered her a job making less then minimum wage. Once again, I was shocked. I tried to call her. She stopped answering any calls from me at all.

She was a huge fan of Ani Difranco and so I called Ani's booking agent to try to get her to play at Dreamworld. She almost did, but something happened and it didn't work out. I did get us tickets to see her in Austin though. When I told Lana that I had gotten us tickets she said "great, just send them down here and I'll take a friend." Of course that seemed strange that she didn't want to see her husband even though she had been gone for a month now. So when I said I wanted to go too, she was disappointed and said "Why don't you just meet me down there and we can watch the show together and then I'll leave." When I insisted that she come up and see me she had a bunch of excuses as to why she had to work until the last second, but she would be there in time to drive to Austin to see the concert.

Oct. 4th we drove down to Austin. She was very distant. Her and the kids had been sick since they had been sleeping out in a tent for the last month on some muddy patch of dirt in Houston. When I asked why she didn't answer any of my calls, she said her cell phone didn't get any reception down there and so she hadn't gotten my calls. I knew she it wasn't true.

The next morning we were driving around running errands with the kids. Lana went in a store by herself and I stayed in the car with the kids. Lily told me that they had been at the place where Brad works the day before and Lily knew lots of details. Sometimes kids make up silly stories, but she knew lots of stuff that was beyond her being able to make it up. She said that Mommy kissed Brad yesterday. I waited until I was alone with my wife and then I asked her about it. I didn't accuse her. I just asked if she had been to his work recently. She lied and said no.

I kept giving her a chance to come clean or tell me it was a misunderstanding or something. Every time I told her a detail she would get more defensive. Then finally she flew off the handle. She said " I thought you said you had forgiven me and you weren't going to bring this up anymore. Why are you trying to pry stuff out of Lily? That isn't fair to her! I'm sick of this! We're leaving!"

She called her dad who drove right over and started packing her stuff up... again. He walked by me and gave me that look that said " I knew you were a scumbag since the first day I met you. I'm so glad Lana finally got a clue and she is leaving you. She deserved better then you anyway." Up to this point I hadn't told anyone what was going on. I had covered for her to save her dignity. I had put up with everyone acting like any problems we had were my fault for long enough.

I looked him dead in the eye and said, " You know she is cheating on me, don't you?" His jaw dropped. He didn't have a clue, or if he did he was a great actor, or maybe he was just surprised that I had actually said it. Then I went on " Oh yeah, she's been getting high, she smokes now, she drinks all the time... If you help her leave me you will be contributing to the destruction of our family." He thought for a moment and I could tell my words struck deep, but then he just pushed me out of the way and started carrying more of her things out.

She left with the kids screaming for their daddy. She left with me crying on our front porch. After the whole painful ordeal I had to pick up the pieces, again. I had a concert that night that I had to fake being happy for. Over the next few months I tried to get her to come back. I tried every way I could think of to get her to come back. Even though she had done all that rotten stuff to me, even though she had betrayed me and desecrated our marriage I still loved her. She didn't answer or return calls. She only called when she needed money. She would be nice long enough to get some money and then she would leave again.

Right before Thanksgiving she said she didn't want to have Thanksgiving with me. On Thanksgiving night, around midnight, her mother called me. She asked why I wasn't doing more to try to get Lana back. She accused me of ruining our marriage and throwing it all away. She went on for about thirty minutes until she finally got to what she was trying to say. Lana had a boyfriend she was living with that she had brought up to Oklahoma for Thanksgiving dinner with their entire family. So, while I had stayed home alone for Thanksgiving she had flaunted her boyfriend that she was having another affair with to her entire family.

The next day Lana came home and acted like nothing had happened. Some guy kept calling her on her cell phone all day long. I knew it was Joel, her boyfriend, but I pretended to not know about it. I wanted her to come clean. I wanted her to tell me the truth. I wanted her to tell me it was a misunderstanding and that she loved me or that she was sorry. I gave her room to do all that... but nothing.

I suggested that this guy that was calling constantly sounded like he was more than a friend. She threw a fit to cover it up. As the conversation went on I let on to more and more details until she finally broke and told the truth... kind of. She said that she was sorry and she cried a lot. She told me that she had slept with 5 different guys within the last 5 weeks and now she was in love with this guy Joel. She said, "I don't know what is the matter with me. I'm sorry. I know that it hurts you. I don't want to ever do it again. I love you and you only."

I guess I just wanted to believe her so I took her back again, like a fool. Deep down I just wanted my family back and I wanted my wife back. That night I had a concert at Dreamworld. I remember vividly a girl that worked my concession stand bragging that someone was going to let her drive their car. I told her not to do it. She giggled and ran off. The show ended and the bands were loading out of the backstage. I was secretly praying to die. River and I were talking on the stage when we heard what sounded like a shotgun going off outside the club.

It was clear enough that no one questioned it. We just ran outside to see what had happened. I ran ahead of everyone else and it was as if the world had just stopped. It wasn't a shotgun blast. It was a car crash right in front of my club. I could see where the car had been hit and thrown at least a hundred feet from the point of impact. The car horn was going off and wouldn't stop. Someone was calling 911 in the background. Everyone seemed panicked. I calmly came up to the vehicle and I saw that there were five people in the car.

The driver was a girl. She looked grey and white and was unconscious. She was folded into the door's twisted metal. I immediately thought "That girl is dead. There is nothing we can do for her now. I should try to help the others." I couldn't help but to feel a little jealous of whoever that girl was. She was getting to go home, right there in front of me. How I wanted to die and just stop the pain." Then I heard my Ronna frantically screaming at the top of her lungs. I was a little frustrated because I thought "this situation is hard enough without you screaming. What is that going to help?"

Then I heard what she was saying "It's Billie! It's Billie! It's Billie!" She kept saying it over and over. I was thinking "No it isn't", but then I turned around. It was like my eyes had to adjust for a second. The driver of the car was Billie. I had just talked to her minutes before. I had just warned her not to drive the car. I looked in the car and I knew everyone in there! It was Derek... and James... and Cody... and Jordan... and Billie, all people from my club. All people I knew and talked to. People I had just seen and talked to and taken for granted.

There was no way to get Billie out. She had become part of the car and besides she was dead. The other kids started coming to and got out of the other end of the car. Then someone yelled, "She has a pulse! She has a pulse!" I thought "No she doesn't. You are dreaming. If she does have one it won't be for long. There is no hope for her."

About that time a cop showed up and starting trying to assess the accident. The next thing we knew there were 7 cop cars, 4 fire trucks, and 3 ambulances surrounding us. They used the Jaws of Life to cut the car open to get Billie out. Somehow they got her out alive and on a stretcher. We noticed a helicopter flying very close and we assumed it was the news, but it just kept getting closer until it landed in the road right in front of Dreamworld. Everyone was put in neck braces and driven off in ambulances. Billie was flown away in the helicopter.

I spent the rest of the night trying to call parents and tell them what had happened to their children. It was a hard night. It was very surreal. James got a concussion and he got banged up pretty good. Jordan got out of the car and hid before the cops got there. Cody got a piece of the windshield lodged a half inch deep into his eye. Derek lost three toes, but they sewed them back on. Billie was a wreck.

The car that hit them hit right into her door and never slowed down. They were going about 80 miles per hour. Billie was in a coma for three months. They had to drill a hole in her head to bleed off pressure because her brain was swelling. She had two huge blood clots in her head. She broke some ribs and punctured a lung and cut her liver. She breathed through a hole in her throat for almost six months while on a respirator. She had stomach surgery. She was in intensive care for almost six months. Everybody thought she would probably die soon. Nobody wanted to say it, but we all knew it was true.

We had all just been to the funeral of another kid from Dreamworld named Thomas. A train hit him. It was sad. He had been in my office the day before the accident, if it was an accident. A lot of people thought it was suicide. No one really knows. We didn't want to have another funeral, but it seemed imminent.

So, I finally went home that night/ morning. I told Lana what had happened. We slept together that night for the last time ever. In the morning she said she had to sort some things out in her mind and get some time alone to clear her head. She said she was going to go to Oklahoma to stay with her grandmother for a few days. So she packed up and took the kids and went to Oklahoma. I had another show that night that I had to do. When I got home that night there was a message on the answering machine from Lana saying happily that she was in Oklahoma and that she would call me in a few days.

First of all I have a cell phone that I ALWAYS keep on me, so why didn't she call my cell phone? Secondly, we had Caller ID and Joel's number showed up. It didn't say his name, but he had called earlier and I knew it was Joel even though Lana had lied so I wrote down the number somewhere. It wouldn't be right if years or months or even weeks or days had passed since she said she wouldn't see him anymore, but it was hours! Literally a few hours passed after she told me how sorry she was and that she would never do it again before she was back in his arms! I called her cell, his cell, and his home phone repeatedly with no response. I knew they were there and I knew they heard me. So I left a message that said, "you have twenty minutes to call me or I am going to find out where he lives and come find you."

I got no response, so I called her parents and found out roughly where he lived. I drove for an hour and a half and got there at 2 am. I saw her car and I was furious and hurt. A sea of mixed emotions filled my heart and mind. I knocked on the door and got no answer for a while. I heard some shuffling around and a few minutes later Joel came to the window of the door. He asked who it was and what I was doing there in the middle of the night. I asked if Lana was there and he said "Yes" at which point I told him that was my wife he was screwing in there. He stalled some more and tried to talk his way out of opening the door, but I got him to open it. I pushed my way in the house. He tried to fight me a little bit, but I think he realized that I was a lot stronger and a lot madder then he was. He kept threatening to call the cops and I kept daring him to do it so he could go to jail.

There was a gun and a bunch of bullets sitting on the washing machine right as I walked in the mobile home. I was thinking a few things. One, why is there a gun and bullets within my children's reach? And two, why is she leaving me for this loser who lives in a trashy trailer behind his parent's trailer? He is a nothing to look at! He is poor! He is irritating! He is a coward! I am none of these things. What is the matter with her? Lana was hiding from me in his bedroom and wouldn't come out. She was terrified. I would be too, I suppose, if I had done what she did. So, I sat and calmly talked to Joel!

I told him that whatever she might have told him that we were married and he was committing adultery with my wife. He didn't care at all. He was proud of it. He gave me some pseudo-intellectual sounding speech about how marriage was just a piece of paper and that Lana and I were already divorced in our hearts and that they were already married in their hearts. Anyone who hides in secret while seducing another man's wife is a coward and scum of the earth. They break hearts and break homes and children. They destroy just so they can get off without obligation.

I guess you never know what is really in you until you are put in that situation. I just didn't think either one of them were worth the hassle. I honestly felt sorry for them. Their punishment was that they had to live with themselves for the rest of their lives.

Finally, Lana agreed to come out and talk to me if I went outside first. I did. Joel came out with her like he was going to protect her from me. He argued for a second and then he went inside. It was windy and cold and dark. So was she. I told her to come home and stop doing this to us. She said "No!" I told her "This is the last chance you get. Come home tonight and never do this again and I won't bring it up again or make your decision tonight to leave me forever." She said, " I don't love you. I love Joel. And I want a divorce!"

Brokenhearted I said "Fine then. It is over. Are you sure that is your decision?" She said, " I don't love you. I love Joel. And I want a divorce!" With tears in my eyes I told her " Tomorrow morning you will get your divorce. Don't ever come back to me begging to get back together. I never want to see you again. I never want to talk to you again. I always loved you." And I turned and walked away. I thought she would call after me, but she didn't. I thought she would call me when I left, but she didn't. I drove away and she didn't care at all.

I think that was one of the lowest points of my life that night. Words can't express how painful that it is to be betrayed by everyone and then be finished off and spit on by the only one on the planet who should stand beside you no matter what. The weight on my soul that night could have sunk a thousand ships. As I was driving, my mind was anywhere but on the road. It was 3am and there was no one out in this little town I was driving through...except the policeman who decided to pull me over.

Most of the times I know why I get pulled over and I know how fast I was going. He looked at me and said, "do you have any idea how fast you were going?" I said "Honestly I don't. I'm sorry" He freaked out and said "72 miles per hour. Do you know what the speed limit is out here?" I reluctantly said "70?" He retorted with "Not at night, it's not! It's 65 at night! What is your hurry, boy?" This cop had actually pulled me over for going two miles over the speed limit while I was going down a hill! Even if it was 65 like he said, I still wasn't going fast enough to get pulled over. I was thinking, "Just shoot me and get it over with. This is unbelievable! All this happens and then I get some speech about going two miles over the speed limit!"

So I told him that I had just caught my wife in bed with another man, that I had seen several of my friends almost die the night before, and that I just wasn't paying attention. He took my license and registration and went back to his car. He must have waited ten minutes before coming back to me. He said, " Well I don't know why you would want a girl like that anyway. If I were you I would leave her! You are a fool. Anyway, are you sure you are safe to drive tonight? I can incarcerate you for the night and you can spend the night in jail if you want."

I assured him that I was fine and didn't need any "favors" like that, but thank you for being so thoughtful. He then warned me that if he ever so much as saw my truck in his town again that he would arrest me himself and that he had other cops ahead of me on my way home that he was going to call and warn them about me. And if I were so much as one mile over I would go to jail tonight! He also reminded me that he was the law in these parts and that they didn't take kindly to folks like me (with long hair). I thanked him and sped on home.

So, when I finally got home I got the chance to do what I had needed to do for way too long now. I got in the shower and I broke down. Not a little. I lost it! I cried my eyes out. I didn't hold back. It was just too much. I couldn't handle it anymore. The cops were falsely accusing me and I would probably be arrested soon. I was $545,000 in debt and I was making absolutely no headway. The Christians hated me because I had secular music in my club. Everyone else hated me because I was a Christian and I didn't sell alcohol. We weren't making any money. I met my real father for the first time in my life and let's face it he was crazy and of no consolation to me. Billie had almost died the night before. A lot of people had been dying recently. The World Trade Center had just fallen a few months before and the world was in turmoil. The recession was killing any hope of my business ever making it. It looked like World War III was about to break out. And, honestly, I could handle all that, but then the only person in the world who was supposed to stand by me had betrayed me... repeatedly. She had cheated and lied and come back and done it again and again and again.

I realize it was pathetic, but I just couldn't take it so I cried. No, I wept bitterly! I was calling out to God and I said " God, please take me home. I won't kill myself, but please take me out of the game. It is too much for me. I can't keep it together. Please take me home! Please let me die! Please have mercy on me and just put me out of my misery. Arrange for a car crash or a lightning bolt or anything you see fit. Just let me come home. Please!" As I lay there crying and feeling sorry for myself on the shower floor I remembered a verse I had read in the Bible a few weeks before in Jeremiah 12. It says: " If you have raced with mere men on foot and they have worn you out, how can you compete with horses? If you stumble in safe country, how will you manage in the thickets by the Jordan?"

And then I took a moment and realized there are people that have it a lot worse than me. I am not the first man to go through this and I won't be the last. At least I'm not in a coma. At least I don't have AIDS. And even if I did, I am not a coward. You see there are no cowards in heaven. And so at that moment on the shower floor I stopped crying. I lifted my head towards heaven and I said, "Well then, I'll run with horses. I'll turn the other cheek. I'll walk the extra mile. I'll be the better man. I'll do miracles. I will believe. Everything I have is borrowed anyway. So, make me what you need, God. I will do whatever you ask. I am yours. I won't feel sorry for myself... I am blessed."

I got myself up out of the shower, got dressed, and I wrote the title song to my first album "I Will Run With Horses." The words are:

I Will Run With Horses

If you feel worn out, tired, and weak when you run with men
How then shall you run with horses?
And if you stumble and fall when you are safe at home
How then shall you stand my son when you are all alone?
And how can you continue in sin and still condemn your brother?
How can you have a beam in your eye and see the speck in another's?

I will stay true, I will stand, I will run with horses
I will believe, I will not fall, by your grace I stand
With my Lord I can do all things, I will run with horses
Even to death I carry my cross, I will fly with angels!

A man is not born a hero, songs about him they do not sing
Until he does something great, until he is amazing
The man stood strong, the man stood tall

He did what was right, he didn't fall
He risked his life, he risked his soul
Against all odds he had hope

I will stay true, I will stand, I will run with horses
I will believe, I will not fall, by your grace I stand
With my Lord I can do all things, I will run with horses
Even to death I carry my cross, I will fly with angels!
Even to death I carry my cross, I will walk with Jesus!

I will stay true, I will stand, I will run with horses
I will believe, I will not fall, by your grace I stand
With my Lord I can do all things, I will run with horses
Even to death I carry my cross, I will fly with angels!
Even to death I carry my cross, I will walk with Jesus!
Even to death I carry my cross, I will run with horses!

The whole next day I spent in the courthouse filing for a divorce. I can't tell you how difficult that was for me. I never wanted to get a divorce. I never planned for it. It seemed that only women worked in the divorce section of the courthouse. Everyone of them gave me that look like "You scumbag why are you doing this to her? You are probably cheating on her... and beating her. You are probably a drug addict loser, etc., etc., etc." I had to go and humbly ask for help.

Of course, no one would help me. They can't give legal advice or they will get fired. All I wanted to know was what floor of the building to go to. Apparently that was considered legal advice to them, or maybe they were just man-haters and thought the worst of me. I didn't try to defend myself. I just wandered around aimlessly until I figured out what to do. It was by far one of the most difficult and humiliating things I have ever had to go through.

Lana signed everything quickly. She was itching to get divorced so that her and Joel could get married. He came along with her to sign papers. He wouldn't get out of the car. The next 50 times I saw her he was always in the car. He never got out. He never said hello. He wouldn't look me in the eye. They deserved each other. My kids didn't deserve any of this though. Kids make divorce harder than anything else. All of the sudden a million questions ran through my head about what I could possibly do to make the whole thing right. The answer is: NOTHING MAKES DIVORCE RIGHT! NOTHING!

There are no easy answers because this isn't the way it is supposed to be. Things like this make BROKEN HOMES! Broken, pretty much, beyond repair. And then to add insult to injury your fate lies in the decision of a stranger (a judge) who listens to each of your stories for a few minutes and decides your family's destiny. The whole thing just seems so wrong. It was finally out of my hands. Sixty-one days later we were divorced, legally. It was like getting a driver's license or a passport. It was completely heartless.

Four days before my divorce was legal I wrote this:

My Prayer

I want a pure heart before you God.
I want to have a clean conscience.
I want to know that I have made your day.
I want to feel you smile down upon me.
I want to thank you for being so kind.
I want to apologize for being so cruel and foolish.
I want to choose right over wrong every time, but I don't.
I want to know you more than anything...
...And not be alone.
I want to bow before you on that day and be proud of what you helped me to do.
I want to rise above. I want to run with horses.

I want to fly with eagles, and be in your presence forever.

I want to know that I didn't miss an opportunity and that I chose wisely.

I want my battles to be worth the struggle and the fight.

I want to take the talents you have given me and use them well, with increase one thousand fold.

I want to be the man you want me to be; strong and courageous, gentle and kind, humble but powerful, honest and upright.

I want to do the right thing no matter the personal cost to myself or my pride.

I want you to brag in heaven about your servant John.

I want to make you proud and put a smile on your face. You are my everything. You are the reason I draw breath.

I owe you a debt I cannot repay, but I will try out of humble gratitude to live a life that will bring you joy and, hopefully make you happy to have me as a son... and a friend.

But the truth is that I settle everyday to be just as everyone else.

I fall. I stumble. I sin.

Of course, I don't want to remember that part, but when I do it helps me to find the grace to forgive those that have sinned against me.

It helps me to remember that even though we I don't deserve anything from you, that you pour your riches and grace on me.

I believe that you are great and because of that I believe that I can be more.

You own the cattle on a thousand hills... and the hills!

For whatever reason you have given me the keys to the kingdom.

I believe you can do anything.

I have no fear of death or anything else for I know that I am in your hands and that when my day is here it will be a joyous one.

You inspire me to love, forgive, and encourage.

I do not know my purpose for I see through a glass dimly, but I do know that you have made me into something beautiful and that I have changed.
My heart is disgusted by sin and yet I still genuinely love the sinners.
I truly enjoy their company with or without any results from evangelism.
I know I am a terrible pray-er so I wanted to write this to help me keep my train of thought and just to say "Thank you."
Help me to be the man that you want me to be.

Divorce is a terrible evil that has broken the spirit of millions of people and done irreparable damage to our country and our world. It has made our daughters into whores and our sons into criminals and murderers. If you think I'm lying, look around you. You won't have to look far. Girls who sleep around are trying to find love and affection from a man, because their father wasn't around. Girls need to feel loved and special and precious and if they don't then, they settle for sex in the hopes that "maybe THIS man will love me."

Boys are furious and lash out. They become troublemakers. They get in fights. They drink, do drugs, join gangs, and become criminals because there isn't a man to lead the way in the right direction. There is no role model in the house. Does everyone react that way? No, perhaps not... as extremely. But I pray every day that my children don't grow up too scarred from my divorce. I pray that they are solid people with good hearts. So, I have resolved to not say anything bad about their mother and to never tell them what she did to me or why I can't be there to kiss them goodnight. Nothing breaks my heart more then watching my two beautiful children grow up without a father around. I have shed many tears for them and spent many hours on my knees praying for them.

One of the other really rotten things about divorce is that you have this ominous feeling of failure. It is overwhelming sometimes. You just feel inadequate and hopeless. I broke down for no reason at all and just started crying every single time I got alone. I would see a child in a car next to me and just start crying uncontrollably.

I am not really emotional. Most people go out and screw everyone they meet after they get divorced. Most people drink or start doing drugs or some self-destructive thing to numb the pain. They fake it, but everyone knows they are miserable. You can spot a divorced person from across a room if you have been through one yourself.

Everyone knew I was miserable, but I didn't do any of those things. I turned my pain into art, and music, and writing. I was honest about my pain and used it to try to help other people who were going through the same things. They are all around you if you pay attention. All of the sudden I had a lot of free time. I had pretty much been a workaholic and I always had a long list of things that were undone, but suddenly I had nothing to do and no one to do it with.

I watched EVERY SINGLE movie that came out in 2002. It was pathetic. It helped me get my mind off my pain for an hour and a half or so. I always went alone. I cried a lot. I sat in the back. I took it hard.? I won't lie to you. My heart was broken, what can I say? Before I went through a divorce myself I know I wouldn't have understood. Once you have been through one though, there is no judgmental attitude. There are no speeches about keeping it together. You see the pain and you know it first hand. All there is left is compassion for that hurting soul.

13 Let the Healing Begin

Right up until the day of my divorce I really thought Lana would come back and apologize and make it right again. She didn't. It was a long hard road uphill that I am honestly still fighting, but I needed to heal and so God provided a way. I had fixed up our house so I could sell it to pay off some of the debt from the club. It sold about a week after the divorce was finalized. While I was at the closing for our house I met a guy that my realtor knew. He went to Grace Community Church which was a little odd because I had helped out up at Grace several years ago when I was a youth pastor.

I asked how everything was going up there and if he knew some of the same people that I did. Sure enough they were still there. I decided to go. I was looking for a new church because everyone at my old church had known Lana and she was all I heard about all the time. I was ready to move on. It was hard to believe I was really single again. Most people would like the idea I suppose, not me. I want someone to come home to, someone to fight for and work for. I want someone to love and someone to love me. It is not good for a man to be alone... that's a quote from God!

So, I walked in to Grace that Sunday and the pastor was giving a sermon on Psalm 23. He explained that he was taking a week for each verse in this chapter, which I honestly didn't think was humanly possible. The verse he was on when I got there was

"Though I walk through the valley of the shadow of death I will fear no evil for you are with me; your rod and your staff they comfort me."

- Psalm 23:4

That hit home for me. I love how God works. He always has an answer to your prayers if you just pay attention and are obedient. The pastor went on to say that the valley of the shadow of death was a real place. King David wrote this before he was a king, back when he was a shepherd boy. As a shepherd he watched his flock and cared for their needs. In the spring he would let the sheep graze in the lowlands, but after a while they would eat most of the grass and so he would have to take them to higher ground. The only way up to the higher ground was to walk them through a deep valley. It was so deep that light couldn't reach the floor of the ravine. That is why it was called the valley of the shadow of death. It was a real place.

The pastor said, "Notice that you haven't taken up residence in the valley, you are going '**through** the valley'. God only let's bad things happen to you to bring you to higher ground and the only way up is through the valley. The sheep would get anxious while they walked through the valley and so the shepherd would talk with them and he would place his staff on them so that they would know that he was there. The sheep knew that David would watch over them and when they knew David was there it would calm them." I'm sure I don't have to explain the object lesson here. God is our shepherd and he is with us, just like David was there with his sheep.

Over the next few weeks he spoke of the rest of the chapter. " You prepare a table before me in the presence of my enemies. You anoint my head with oil; my cup overflows. Surely goodness and mercy will follow me all the days of my life, and I will dwell in the house of the Lord forever." Psalm 23: 5-6

The object lesson goes on. Before David would let the sheep into the lush pastures in the higher ground he would have to make sure it was safe. He would take his staff and poke around for snake holes. He would pour oil in the snake holes. If he didn't do this than the adder snakes would bite the faces of the sheep while they were grazing. The adder snakes didn't like the smell of the oil and so they would stay away from the hole if it had oil on it.

As an added safety precaution he would "anoint" the sheep's heads with oil. This way the snakes would stay away from the sheep even if David missed some snake holes. There were also nose flies that would go into the sheep's noses and lay eggs. It would drive the sheep crazy. However the nose flies didn't like the smell of the oil either. And so David literally prepared a table before his sheep in the presence of their enemies (the snakes and the nose flies). What a beautiful analogy!

Sheep don't like to get their noses wet. David would go to great lengths to keep their water troughs overflowing so they wouldn't have to get their faces wet trying to drink the water. Even though this was more hassle for him he loved his sheep and wanted the best for them and this was just one more way to show it. God was looking out for me in this way as well. He prepared a table before me in the presence of my enemies. My cup overflowed. How can I complain when my God goes to such great lengths to make sure I am looked after? How blessed am I? Very!

I kept going to church at Grace and I still do. My pastor is always right on to what I need to hear. It is amazing! I listen intently and take his sermons with me every week. I am sure he doesn't know this about me. Maybe he will read this and know what a difference he has made in my life?

So, right around this time we had a Christian wrestling group come out to the club and perform. Some guys with a video camera came out and set up some lights. They filmed the whole thing. They interviewed me because I was the venue owner. I did the interview. I've done lots of interviews. Apparently, these guys were doing a documentary on this wrestling group. It looked low budget, but I knew there were still costs so I asked who they worked for. They said they were making it independently and then they hoped to sell it to one of the major TV stations or cable channels. So, I asked if there was enough money in something like that to justify all their costs.

They told me the numbers and River and I had a meeting that night. We were going to make some TV, or movies, or something. We were smart enough and talented enough. But what would we do? We thought realistically and brainstormed. Drama? No. Not us. Sci-fi? No. We didn't have a budget and we weren't nerds. Action? I would love to, but no budget. Comedy! Yeah, now that I can do!

But what would we write about? We brainstormed some more. We were driving through the parking lot at Dreamworld. People in groups are not exceptionally intelligent and River said why don't you make a movie about these stupid, stupid people? I liked the thought and so I wrote a movie script entitled "Stupid, Stupid People". It took eight days for me to write. Is it good? No, it is stupid! That's the point. But it is funny. It is all about this club called Dreamworld that I own and all the stupid things that go on there. Almost everything in the movie has actually happened in some context. I have changed names, a little. I have exaggerated stuff, a lot. It is horrible. I loved making it.

So, then I bought a camera and some editing software, and a better computer. You wouldn't think making a movie would be that hard. It really isn't. It is a lot of fun! I love it! Writing is fun. Filming is fun. Acting is fun. Editing is fun. The whole process is just fun. I feel blessed just getting to be involved at all.

I already told you about my song " I Will Run With Horses." When I bought my editing software (Adobe Premiere 6.0) it had a picture on the cover of horses running out of the front of a video camera. I didn't look twice, but my director Shaun said "Look, I Will Run With Horses! You were made for this!" I felt very special. God had made me for a reason.

I figure everyone gripes about how bad our entertainment is, but they don't do anything to try to change it. Either pick up your load and do your part or please stop complaining. As for me, I will do my part AND I won't complain. I love people. I love art and music and movies. I love to entertain and to be entertained. I will do it whether or not there is a payoff. I love it! I will run with horses!

A few friends of mine gave me some books to read that they said had helped them. One of the books talked about the process of grieving. According to the book, going through a divorce is like losing a loved one. It's like someone you loved died. The steps are: shock, denial, anger, depression, and acceptance, and hopefully forgiveness. You have to go through all these to completely heal. Some people never let themselves go through these steps and so they never heal. I went through all of them.

When I first found out about Lana cheating I was definitely in shock. Then I was in denial for a while. I thought everybody must all be wrong about her or maybe this was some sick joke or something. Then I was angry. I am glad I didn't hurt someone during all that because I could have easily hurt a lot of people. Fortunately, I had some self-control and I think things through before I act them out.

Then I was depressed... for a long time! I heard it takes one week of grieving for every six months you were together. We were together for a little over 9 years, so that would be 18 weeks of grieving (four and a half months). It was almost exactly that long for me. I wrote a lot of songs about my pain. I didn't hide it. I was honest with anyone who asked. I think it was very therapeutic for me and hopefully helped some other people out with their pain as well. If other people can't learn from my mistakes than my pain is a waste.

I made an entire CD since I owned a recording studio and all. I have written several hundred songs, but this was the first full CD I had recorded. A lot of people seemed to like it and I think God used it to help heal a lot of them. I don't mind being the first to stand up and say I have been hurt and I have done wrong. Confession is a beautiful thing. Here are words to some of the songs on this CD.

Crushed

I've been smitten; I've been wronged,
I know more pain then I've ever known before,
The wound I carry knows no healing,
The cross I bear is unyielding pain,
I don't know how I find the strength to make it through the day,
And I don't know how I hold my head up to fake a smile,
You don't know the weight of the burden I carry,
You don't know how it crushes me,

Perhaps you know how it feels to hear the words that smother you,
Perhaps you know how it feels when your heart dies,
When you'd rather be dead than alive,
Nothing matters when you've lost everything,
Nothing matters to me,

I forgive you my love,
And I lay down all rights I have,
You are beautiful in my eyes,
Come and join me in eternal life,
May the sun always shine upon you,
May everything you touch be blessed,
I forgive you my love,
And I lay down all rights I have,
You are beautiful in my eyes,
Come and join me in eternal life

Time Well Spent

Lord you know me from head to toe,
You know where I come and when I go,
You know my inmost being and my sin,
Lord I know that you respect no one,
There is no one righteous, no not one,
We all like sheep, we have gone astray,
And when the night makes my head clear,
And I sense that you are very near,
And your honesty it stops all the lies,
Who am I?
Lord I am yours from head to toe,
I am yours wherever I go,
I know that you will never leave,
I know that you, you love me!

Lord sometimes I lose my way,
I think of all the bills I have to pay,
And all the things I have to do,
Instead of love you,
And Lord sometimes I build a shrine,
Because I cannot find the time,
To spend alone with you in prayer,
So I act like I don't care,
But Lord our time together is sweet,
I shed tears as I'm on my knees,
And just as soon I forget,

Oh Lord, how I long to be home,
With temptation and sin very far gone,
Sometimes this burden crushes me,
I long to be free!

And son, don't you know I love you, don't be so hard,
Soon you'll be home,
And tears of joy stream down my face when I see your
faith,
I leap from my throne,
And son, I know it's hard to walk the extra mile, but
you're love is bold,
And I've got such a party waiting for you; it'll never be
through,
Soon you'll be home,
Soon you'll be home

<u>*Home At Last*</u>

My eyes have seen their share of pain, and my hands
have worked hard
My feet have walked the extra mile, and my face turned
the other cheek
And I have run tirelessly, and my heart is scarred
And my spirit's humble and I am meek

For my life it is a battlefield, and I have run just like he
planned
I stand strong, and I stand bloody, and I stand weak,
but I do stand!
For one day I will leave here, this prison I call my
home
And I will not look back and I will not cry, but tears of
joy... for I am home

You can mock and you can laugh at me, and you can
kill me and you can steal
But you cannot take my spirit and my soul you cannot
steal

And you cannot take away my dignity and you cannot take me from my home
I do not fear, I will not be afraid, you cannot take what I don't give

For not one day has escaped me without me begging for it to be my last
That's right, I said
NOT ONE DAY HAS ESCAPED ME WITHOUT ME BEGGING FOR IT TO BE MY LAST!
I have died, but I'm not alone, for I know God and his son
And I have taken a beating, and I have lost some, but Hallelujah! I have won!

Hallelujah! I'm finally home, Hallelujah! I am free!
Hallelujah! I'm finally home, Hallelujah! I am free!
No more pain and no more tears, no more death I'm finally free!
No more pain and no more tears, no more death I'm finally free!
Hallelujah! I'm finally home, Hallelujah! I am free!
Hallelujah! I'm finally home, Hallelujah! I am free!

I Know Pain, I Know Sorrow

Close your eyes if but for a moment,
I know that you do not have much time,
Two thousand years ago, yes you remember,
God hung clothed in flesh, died for your sins and mine,
He marched as a criminal to Calvary,
Mocked and beaten then we nailed him to the tree,
Are you still blind my child, can you not see?
Your sin nailed him there, but he rose to free,

I know that it has been hard for you lately my child,
I know pain, I know sorrow, I know love,
Even in the valley I'll be there with you,
I am able to deliver you, so be strong,

God, it feels like I'm in the desert,
Been here forty days and going on forty nights,
The devil's closing in to devour,
I don't have much strength; I think I'm going to die,

Wait, a shaft of light! Yes there I see it,
The end is near; the tunnel is not so deep,
There is someone who has been here before me,
He knows the way; yes he has eyes to see,

I know that it has been hard for you lately my child,
I know pain, I know sorrow, I know love,
Even in the valley I'll be there with you,
I am able to deliver you, so be strong,

Think it not strange when you walk the path of sorrows
our Lord has trod,
We all have our share of burdens; we must all carry
our cross,
And I bear my share of scars from a battle, how can I
sleep?
When it seems like the enemy is closing in we need to
get down on our knees,
And I bear no shame when I preach in Jesus' name

I learned a lot of lessons through my divorce. I learned how much one person could hurt another one by their betrayal. It would have been different if she had been a stranger. I could almost justify it away and say that she didn't know me. But we had spent years together. We knew everything about each other. We had children together. And she went behind my back and betrayed me and went back on her word. It hurt. More than I can ever explain. Then I realized that we do the same thing to God every day.

We come back and apologize and say we are sorry. We cry and beg forgiveness. We make excuses, but we don't really repent. We don't really change. I realized how much we break God's heart every day. I knew the terrible pain of one man from one woman who was unfaithful, but God knows the pain of billions of people that He knows intimately breaking His heart every day!

It made me want to be a better man. It made me want to do my part at least to give joy to the God that gave me everything. I realized that He isn't impressed with our money or our "sacrifices". After all we are only giving back what he gave us in the first place. A sacrifice that doesn't cost you anything is not a sacrifice at all, and let's face it most of our "sacrifices" cost us nothing.

I realized that all God wants from us is love, companionship, and obedience. That is not hard. He just loves us and wants to spend time with us. Sometimes you know someone loves you, but you just want to hear them say it. Sometimes they say it, but you want them to mean it. Sometimes people's actions are the exact opposite of what they say and they are blind to it. I wrote this song, because it breaks my heart to see God's heart broken. I want to be better than that. I want to put it in writing. It's simple, but powerful and true.

No one Left?

Is there no one left who can see through the eyes of God?
Is there no one left with a heart?
Is there no one with any sense of compassion beyond their own agenda?
Is there no one?
And it must break your heart to see the sin reign in this land
It is hard pressed down and overflowing!
For if I had my way I'd burn this place right to the ground

I'd spare no one, no, not even me!
But thank you, you are beautiful beyond imagination;
you are my Lord and king
Behold the Lamb of God who takes away the sins of
the world, you're why I sing
But who will, who will tell them Lord? Here I am!
Please send me!
For when I close my eyes for the last time
Oh Hallelujah! It's you and me

For when I close my eyes for the last time
Oh Hallelujah! It's you and me   (repeat)

This Lonely Heart

One day this lonely heart will beat no more,
Oh what a happy and glorious morn',
For though my body has met the greatest pain on
earth,
And to death I have fallen,
My soul is now with the Lord and I am now in heaven!

My time on earth is over; the veil has been lifted,
The two who were divided now meet,
My Lord and I, we talk face to face,
He says my son was that such a feat?

For we have forever, you are mine and I am yours,
And by the way "Well done with your chores",
I know it wasn't easy, but was it really hard?
After all I was with you all the while

The Road To Hell

Today I went and I visited the house. Of Satan,
He knew my name!

This is not the first time,
He knew my inmost desire,
He knew right what I needed and he touched me there
again,
I know there is a price to pay,
He'll feast upon my soul one day,
I don't think I'm all that bad,
I can leave anytime I want to,
But I kind of like it here,
And where would I go?

I gave away my soul for nothing,
I have got no soul to sell,
I'll spend forever burning,
I have run the road to hell!

But everyday my fix gets bigger, the rush gets smaller,
The price goes up, and I need it more,
And everyday I wonder a little more why
I came here in the first place
I don't know why
Oh-oh oh-oh oh

I gave away my soul for nothing,
I have got no soul to sell,
I'll spend forever burning,
I have run the road to hell!

Lately I've noticed that my chain doesn't seem quite as
long,
Lately I've noticed that my dose doesn't seem quite as
strong,
And that the hollowness in my heart is full,
And I don't care about anything anymore,
And I feel that I don't have too long to go

I can't move... I can't speak... the time is now... he's
come for me!
"Wait, NO! Remember we are friends,
That hurts, that burns, that doesn't bend!"

I never thought it would come to this, I thought you loved me
You lie, but I believed

I read an interesting book that inspired this song. It comes from Mark 11: 12-26 which says "the next day as they were leaving Bethany, Jesus was hungry. Seeing in the distance a fig tree, he went to find out if it had any fruit. When he reached it, he found nothing but leaves, **because it was not the season for figs**. Then he said to the tree, 'May no one ever eat fruit from you again.' And his disciples heard him say it...

In the morning, as they went along, they saw the fig tree withered from the roots. Peter remembered and said to Jesus, 'Rabbi, look! The fig tree you cursed has withered!'
'Have faith in God,' Jesus answered, 'I tell you the truth, if anyone says to this mountain, Go throw yourself into the sea, and does not doubt in his heart but believes that what he says will happen, it will be done for him. Therefore I tell you, whatever you ask for in prayer, believe that you have received it, and it will be yours. And when you stand praying if you hold anything against anyone, forgive him, so that your father in heaven may forgive you your sins."

I had never really thought about the fact that it **wasn't fig season** when Jesus cursed this fig tree. It seems unjust that He would curse a tree for not having fruit when it wasn't even the season for fruit **and** none of the other trees had fruit either. It then brought up the fact that there has never been, nor will there ever be a season where we as people all follow God and do the right thing. There isn't a time when everyone will love each other. **It doesn't matter what everyone else is doing**. The question is "Am I doing what I should be doing?" Jesus always calls us to better then the norm. He calls us to rise above, to turn the other cheek, to love our enemies, to walk the extra mile. These things are not normal. Everyone else is **not** doing them. It is hard. It takes more of a man to turn the other cheek than it does to lash out and retaliate. It takes more of a man to stand up and do the right thing when you know you are standing alone then just to follow the crowd. I realized an incredible lesson and then I wrote this song.

The Fig Tree

On a hill, not alone,
surrounded by no fruit on every side,
The season for love may never come,
Don't want to stand out alone...I will wait

One day my Lord will come for me,
Surely someone will let us know,
They've been saying that for years,
Maybe one day I'll choose to grow...but you first

Oh wait, here he comes for me,
Now there is no time for fruit to grow,
He looks inside this leafy tree, he's hungry,
But there is no good fruit on this soul...Oh no!

I am the fig tree, the fig tree it is me,
In a world where God's season never came,
I never let God grow in me,

Bitterness has overcome,
There is nothing good upon me,
So now I die with everyone,
Withered from the root of my tree,
Never to live again,

I am the fig tree, the fig tree it is me,
In a world where God's season never came,
I never let God grow in me,

So learn a lesson from me,
Stripped of what I thought me to be,
Swiftly run to the light ahead,
Swiftly run to the light ahead

After being single for quite some time, I realized that I didn't want to be alone. I knew that I had a choice in a spouse. We all do. It wasn't something I wanted to think about, but if you fail to plan than you plan to fail. So, I thought long and hard about it. Please, don't think my way is right for everyone. I know myself and I know my weaknesses. I have seen my mistakes and I wanted to not make the same ones again. I know that I am not a type of guy. I am an individual. There is no one else like me. If you cut my life up into pieces everyone would be able to relate to at least something in my life, but I am a strange mix and I know that.

These are the things I wanted in a girl: I didn't want a drug addict, a drunk, or a smoker. I didn't want someone with a potty mouth. I didn't want a girl with kids (Sorry girls, nothing personal. Yes, I know that makes me a hypocrite since I have kids.) I had gotten a vasectomy so that meant the girl had to be OK with not having kids... ever. That isn't easy to find. I wanted someone who was trustworthy. I wanted someone who wouldn't cheat on me.

I wanted someone who loved God, truly. I wanted someone who had experienced some pain. I wanted someone who would love me and appreciate me. I wanted someone I wasn't embarrassed to have around me in public and who wasn't embarrassed by me either. I wanted someone who was intelligent, but not irritating. I wanted someone who was fun, but responsible. I just really wanted someone to share my life with so we could enjoy each other's company. That doesn't seem so hard does it? HaHaHaHaHaHaHaHaHaHaHa!!!!

That is like looking for a needle in a haystack. Throw in the fact that I have long hair, a struggling business with mountains of debt, I live in a one bedroom apartment, I drive a truck with no air conditioning, I eat out for every single meal, I have NO FOOD at all in my apartment ever, I am divorced with two kids and child support checks to think about, I am clearly a workaholic, I am overly spiritual, I like 80's metal music, I play lame acoustic music, I have become a computer nerd, I sleep all day and go out every night of the week, I spend money like water (about $1,000 a day, granted that is mostly business expenses but still), I tell the stupidest jokes in the world, I have no inhibitions at all, I am a thrill seeker, I have no fear, and I have an unhealthy desire to die... and all of the sudden I am asking for the impossible in a girl.

Plus, I am old, fat, ugly, stupid, boring, bald, mean, and short. Some people argue with me about that last statement. Probably because I am not old compared to The Grand Canyon. I am not fat compared to a sumo wrestler. I am not ugly compared to a warthog... that is actually debatable. I am not stupid compared to someone who drinks gas on a regular basis. I am not boring compared to watching paint dry for a week or so. I am not bald compared to Dr. Evil's cat. I am not mean if you compare me to Hitler. And finally, I am not short compared to an ant. Everything is relative I guess. Either way the odds were stacked against me.

I figured I would wait for the right girl instead of just settling for the first girl that said yes. So, I buckled down and got ready to wait... forever! In the meantime I wrote this song to remind me what I was looking for.

Beautiful Soul

I am looking for someone, someone with a beautiful soul
But alas, she is rare, like a precious jewel, she eludes me
Her heart it glows, She is somewhere!
And humility clothes her; her beauty shines wherever she goes
But alas, until I find my beautiful soul, until I find my love...I walk alone

And she can hold her head up high, and she knows no shame
For she has paid the price, my Lord knows her name
Her heart it glows, She is somewhere!
And I am proud to walk beside, and I trust her with my heart and soul
But alas, until I find my beautiful soul, until I find my love...I walk alone

So I will save myself, so I will be true
So I'll be upright, I'll be the man you'd want from me
My heart it glows, She is somewhere!
And I know that I am nothing, I know I am but a stranger to you
But alas, until I find my beautiful soul, until I find my love...I walk alone

She is somewhere!
She is somewhere!
She is somewhere!
But alas, until I find my beautiful soul, until I find my love...I walk alone

It was so weird to think about being with someone besides my, now, ex-wife. It was surreal to think that I was divorced. I got hit on a lot by girls. At first I was shocked. I got hit on when I was married, but I could just point at my ring and say, "I am married." Now that I was a club owner I had hot girls hitting on me all the time and I wasn't married. I was VERY single… and lonely. I just couldn't bring myself to take advantage of any of these girls.

So many of them were addicts and drunks that it was easy to say no. I was looking for a certain girl that God had prepared for me and I was willing to wait. I got good at being polite and still saying no. Most of the time if a girl started getting the least bit serious I would just let them get to know me and they would leave on their own. It wasn't too hard. Most girls wait for the guy to make the first move anyway. When enough time had passed and I hadn't made a move yet they would just move on.

I became a master at the art of superficial relationships, not just with girls... with everyone! I had to have thirty second conversations with all the people that came out to my club and make them all feel special, but still make time for the other couple hundred people out there that night. I NEVER called anyone, but I answered every call. I NEVER e-mailed anyone, but I answered a hundred or so e-mails a day. I NEVER said we should go out and do Blah Blah Blah, but every night I was out doing something fun and exciting. Underneath it all I was very lonely. I was hollow and empty. I smiled all the time. I made the best of it, but I was hurting inside.

I put all my free time (and I had lots of it) into making art. I was making "Stupid, Stupid People" which was a blast. I met a lot of people and made a lot of connections. I wrote a second script called "Job". It is a modern-day story of Job from the Bible, with a "Vanilla Sky- Matrix" type twist in it. I wrote that screenplay in four days. I wrote several other screenplays. I made a cartoon movie. I learned how to do 3-D animation and special effects, which is fun. I learned all types of computer software. I learned everything I could. I love to learn. I started making music videos for bands. I made some connections and got some of them on TV. I got to be in a few commercials and ads. I got in a few movies, which is fun. And I wrote a LOT more songs.

At some point I figured out that I was finally over my divorce and that I had moved on. Lana came back and tried to get back together with me several times, but it was only for the money and security. I told her no. Most people would be happy to watch their ex grovel and beg. I just felt sorry for her, but not enough to take her back. There is a point where you can't go backwards, and she passed that point with me.

I guess I am a jerk. I just don't want to go through that again. I don't get to see the kids much, which hurts a lot. She lives in another town and our schedules conflict. My kids don't seem to miss me that much, which I guess is good. It does break my heart. I know that she is a much better parent than me and so I leave it alone. Plus, I gave her my word that I wouldn't fight her for the kids. Any time I can see Lily and Ben is a blessing and I cherish it. I won't say anything bad about her to them. They have to respect their mother. They have to look up to her and love her. I'm sure one day they will figure out what happened, but it won't be from me.

Over the next year or so I grew a lot. I look back on the songs I wrote and it is very empowering. For example:

I Don't Walk Between The Raindrops

And so there is no confusion,
so there is no misquoting of me
I question everything,
I have explored all the options, but I believe
That I am not my own, I have seen the other side...
and I'm not afraid
So when they burn my body,
do not cry for me for I am home
Yes, I am home

And I have no regrets,
for my heart is pure before the one that saved my soul
I close my eyes, I drink it in, it's no surprise,
I live my life to the full
But I don't walk between the raindrops,
I bleed when I fall, and I cry alone
My heart lies where my treasure is, make no mistake.
Take all I have, take all I am,
but I'm not gone, for I am home

And when I've fought my last battle,
and when the final race has been run
I will sing with the angels, I will fly,
I will talk with kings
I will lay my treasures down.
I will lay them down with my crowns...
along with my chains
But when I gaze upon your face,
what I have lived and died for, it all melts away
For I am home

"The Power Of One"

I saw the great men fall and I saw the world fall with
them,

I saw them led astray and I saw all of us follow them,
I heard their ears tickled with lies and I saw the sin in
our eyes,
I saw the darkness fall; I saw the evil rise,
I stood in agreement with endless compromise,

Is there no man brave enough to
stand up to this darkness?
Is there no man who will deliver us from this pain?
Is there no man who'll risk it all
and just fight back for once?
Does anyone want to go home? Are you tired of it all?
Does anyone even know how to get home at all?

So God heard our cry and
He called the great men home,
"No thanks we're too busy, we'll do it on our own,"
On and on down the chain He went
right down to the least of us,
Until a young man heard His call
and he stepped out from the crowd,
I hear you calling me; will no man lead us home?
I will stand with you even if I stand alone.

So the crowd stood in awe
as they watched the boy walk home alone,
And his path was lit up like the morning sun,
He smiled with dignity, but a tear swelled in his eye,
Will I walk home alone and leave my friends to die?
One by one they followed him, two by two they come,
Until thousands walked beside him, oh the power of
one!

Is there no man brave enough
to stand up to this darkness?
Is there no man who will deliver us from this pain?
Is there no man who'll risk it all
and just fight back for once?
One by one they followed him, two by two they come,
Until thousands walked beside him,

Oh the power of one!

Where is this Man Today?

Do you think that I'm a fool? Do you think I'm blind?
Do you really think that I can't see you?
I know that I am surrounded ten thousand to one,
Does that mean I should turn tail and run from you?
And yes I saw all those beside me flee,
And yes I looked around me, and yes I am alone.
But there are no cowards in heaven and so
I look you dead in the eye and say, "Bring it on!"

And the fight begun

And where is this man today?
And where are the men that fear no man?
And will we run? Or will we fall?
Or will we cower?
Or will we finally stand?
And I have waited long enough,
And I have watched from the corner,
and I have lived a lie.
But never again I say to you
will I stand by and let you win,
Mark my words, I'd rather die!

And the fight went on

And though the lion and the bear roar in my face,
I'll have you know I will not falter,
And though the vultures circle overhead,
and all hope is gone,
They've come, they've come to watch it.
And though I swim with sharks in rough waters,
And the depths they pull me down, they pull me in,
And though the odds are stacked against me
and I'm sure to fall,

I will not fear, I will not yield to sin

And the fight went on
And the fight went on
And the fight went on...

You see God only breaks us down to lift us back up. When I remodeled houses. We took the ugliest parts of the house and gutted them. We ripped them out and we made something new and beautiful. By the time we were done what had been the ugliest parts of the house had become the most beautiful parts of the house. And so it is with God and us. Apparently, I needed to be remodeled and so he let me be torn down so I could be built back better. Thank God that I let Him. Hard times in life can make us better or they can make us bitter. I chose to let them make me better. Thank God that he remodeled my whole house instead of just part of it. He broke me down to nothing, but not without purpose. Even the things that I thought were bad were only for my good.

"And we know that in <u>ALL</u> things God works for the good of those that love Him, who have been called according to His purpose."
- Romans 8:28
If you have a minute read the rest of that chapter. It all applies. In fact, put this book down and stop reading about me. Pick up your Bible and read it instead. That is where the answers are! Believe me, any hope I had, any strength I had, any perseverance I had was only because I was firmly grounded in the Word of God and because I was in it every day.

Let me ask you, how many songs can you sing along to? How many movies can you quote? How many TV shows do you know? How many books have you read? How many hours have you spent studying in your life? Have you actually taken the time to read the whole Bible? Not many have, unfortunately.

Amazing, isn't it? We cling to the things that matter the least and abandon our only hope. Are we fools? People say you can't take it with you go so why bother trying. You are right you can't take material things with you like your money, your debt, your house, your things, your car, and your clothes. In heaven I don't need money because everything is free, and the debt... you can have it if you want. I am happier without it thank you very much. I don't want my apartment in heaven because I have a mansion waiting for me built by the Master Carpenter. In heaven I don't need the things I need here or the clothes or the car. You see heaven is better than anything I can imagine. So, no. I can't take the trash from this world with me. You can have it all, my empire of dirt.

However, all the things that really matter, I CAN take with me. I can take my faith, my love for my fellow man and for God, I can take my dignity, my heart, my soul, my memories, my strength of character. I can take all the things that actually matter. Yes, I can take them with me. Hallelujah!

So why don't we focus more on the eternal? Do we really not believe? Do we really not think that what we do matters? In James it says that faith without works is dead, just like the body without the soul. If you have ever seen a dead body you know that a body without a soul is worthless. There is nothing there but the memory of someone who is now gone.

Without putting our faith into action our faith is like a corpse, worthless and cold. Is it hard to put our faith into action and step out and be different? Yes, of course. Anything worth having is hard to acquire. Is it impossible? Absolutely not. I am a wretch. I am a fool. I was a drug dealer, a liar, an adulterer, a thief, and almost every other bad thing a man can be and yet God made me into something beautiful. You see, the old me has died and I am a new creation. I am perfect in God's sight. I am NOT a wretch or any of those other things anymore. I have been washed whiter than snow. My sins are as far from me as the East is from the West.

Take the time to read your Bible. Then do something revolutionary and actually apply it to your life! You will not regret it. Whatever it is you are aiming towards you must believe that eventually you will get there. Educate yourself while you still have the chance. Look at the trajectory of your life and see where it is you are headed. If you don't like the direction you are going than turn around and change your course. You can do it! Go with God! I'll see you on the other side.

14 Letting Go

My life is full of object lessons for me to learn from. Hopefully, you can learn from my mistakes and my victories so it won't all be in vain. I could go on and on and never shut up about all the ways God has revealed Himself to me and blessed me and taught me. The beautiful thing about God is that He speaks to each one of us in our own language. Not just English or French, or Chinese, but individually. When God speaks to my heart it is not in some foreign way. He brings to my attention flashes of things I have experienced and then weaves them together into another lesson for me.

A year and a half went by after my divorce. I grew. I learned a lot. I feel like a better, stronger man because of what I went through. I feel blessed beyond explanation. My heart overflows. I don't even have to try to encourage people, it just happens. If you spend lots of time with God, you don't have to say anything at all to people. They can see it all over you. There is something different about you. You glow!

After building an entire new website for 17 hours straight I went home tired one night. It was only midnight and so I wasn't sleepy tired, just exhausted. No one was awake and there was nothing to do, so I parked and went for a walk down to the park. I prayed there for about an hour or so. It is nothing new. I pray all the time.

In the middle of it all I said to God " God you know my heart. You know that I want to sell Dreamworld and do movies. I know that if it is against your will for this to happen that I could have a 'For Sale' sign with flashing neon in front of Dreamworld and there could be 100 able, interested, and rich people right across the street that wouldn't see the sign because you would blind their eyes to it. On the other hand, if it is your will then there could be only one person on the face of this earth who would be right for Dreamworld and they could live on the far side of the world, but you could bring them to me. Nevertheless, I don't want to waste my time chasing my own dreams. I would rather be obedient. I don't want to get in the way of your will. So, if I am to own Dreamworld for the rest of my days than I will do it with a smile and to the best of my ability. I only want your will. My will is short-sighted and selfish."

I walked home and felt much better. As I was walking home music was playing on a speaker in front of a business. I walked by at the exact moment that the song said

**"Now John at the bar is a friend of mine
He gets me my drinks for free
And he's quick with a joke or to light up your smoke
But there's someplace that he'd rather be
He says, "Bill, I believe this is killing me."
As the smile ran away from his face
"Well I'm sure that I could be a movie star
If I could get out of this place..."**

-The Piano Man, Billy Joel

That was so weird, but I am used to weird stuff in my life. It was my name and my story on the first song I heard after praying that prayer. I went to bed. A few hours later my grandfather called me from Connecticut and said "John you are in the New York Times!" I was tired so I didn't react much, but later it hit me. I had asked God to bring someone from the far side of the world to me and now he had provided a way for them to come to me.

Why is it that when you finally just give up and let go that God gives you the desires of your heart? Because He wants to know that he is more important to you than any of these other things. He wants us to know we can live without them, but we can't live without Him. I know I can live without them. I can live on nothing. My God watches out for me and provides for me. I am not afraid. So, that is my life in a nutshell so far. This is only the beginning though. I have a lot of adventures ahead of me. You see eternal life starts now. Death is only a door we go through to get to higher ground.

So, however my life plays out here you must know that my faith is NOT shaken. It is encouraged. I have been broken for my own good to be lifted and built back up better than before. I am blessed beyond words. I may not have an earthly father who has ever been there for me, but my real father is the King of Kings!

You see, I am royalty! I am here to learn. I am here to be made better. I am here to help whom I can. I am here to be the hands and feet of my Master. Whether I die tonight or ten thousand years from now I belong to God and to Jesus Christ His son who paid the highest price in the world to save my soul.

I wrote this book for two reasons:

One. Everyone kept saying you really should write a book about your life. So to all of you who said that, here it is. You asked for it. And two. God doesn't light a candle to hide it under a bushel. He doesn't put a city on a hill to be hidden. And He doesn't do miracles in our life so that we will shut up about them. Miracles are meant to be told and my life is a huge string of miracles. I wish I had the time to tell them all to you.

If you look around you will see God's signature on EVERYTHING! From the least to the greatest. If you just look He is there, smiling down on you. You see, God loves you! That is what I am trying to tell you. I'm not blessed because I have a lot of cool things or a club or a recording studio. I am not blessed because I can make movies or write or act or sing or play the guitar or piano. These things are all nice too, but the reason I am blessed is because of Him. The one who walks beside me knows the way home. He made this place and He loves me. That is why I am blessed! Sit in the stillness and you will see that He loves you as well. Do you believe that?

This is another song I wrote. It is simple, but true.

"I'm Coming Home!"

I'm coming home; I'm coming home,

One day this heart will beat no more,
One day I will give my last breath to the Lord,
One day I will close my eyes forever… to this world,
Do not cry for me; do not cry for me,
I am not afraid,

I'm coming home, I'm coming home!

So when they lie about me,
And when they crucify me,
And when they disgrace my very name,
Do not cry for me; do not cry for me,

I am not afraid,

I'm coming home, I'm coming home!

And when I walk in that door
There will be no introductions,
They know my name,
They know my deeds,
They know who I am,

I'm coming home, I'm coming home!

And when the wind whispers softly
And gently brushes your skin,
And when the air in the stillness
Seems to sing to you from within,
I am there with you, and I love you, and I love you
...And I love you!

I don't want you to read this book and think John Tunnell is anything special. **I want you to read this book and know that YOU are special!** If I can do it so can you. You can do anything you set your mind to. We can push a few buttons on a cell phone and talk to anyone on the planet in real time because someone believed it could be done and they didn't stop trying until it was done. We can take the beating heart out of a man and replace it with the heart of a dead man and he can live. Why? Because someone believed it could be done and didn't give up until it was done. We have done amazing things because someone believed it could be done and didn't give up until it was so.

If you measure what we eat, drive, live in, and how we communicate we have grown exponentially over the last several years. If you measure the way we treat each other or our faith we are going at a snail's pace at best. I am not satisfied with that. Not on my watch. Not without a fight. We are better than that. Try reading the Bible and then apply it to your life. Try turning the other cheek, walking the extra mile, loving your enemies. Spread your wings and fly for once. Run with horses. Fly with angels!

One day I will have to give an account for my life. One day I will have to stand not only before God, but also before all of you. I will have to stand next to Peter and Paul and John and Steven and all the disciples and all the martyrs that gave their lives. I will stand next to saints who were torn in two, who were fed to the lions, who were tortured for their faith. I will stand in the midst of prophets and apostles. What will my excuse be? I was too tired or lazy or busy or afraid to speak? NO! There is no excuse to give that is adequate. I want to live without excuses. I want to live a righteous life. You will be thankful if you do the same.

And finally I want to thank all of you. This book is more about you than it is about me. I am merely a collage of what I have learned from all of you. I don't have a single original thought. If there is anything good in me, it has come from you.

I would write acknowledgements, but that has been what this whole book is. I wanted to acknowledge all of you that lifted my spirits, that challenged me, that prayed for me, that kept me in line. I wanted to thank all of you countless kind individuals who haven't yet been thanked by me. **Thank you for seeing potential in a wretch like me.**

I was not worth it, but thank you anyway. You have meant the world to me. You give me wings to fly and a voice to speak. You have given me a heart of flesh, instead of a heart of stone. If I were to die tonight I would be completely content with my life. Thank you. Thank you. Thank you. Thank you. One thousand times thank you. You will never know what a difference you made to me. I am in your debt forever.

- John Tunnell

65970143R00151

Made in the USA
San Bernardino, CA
07 January 2018